Little Hillbillies of Nantahala

BERT BATEMAN

Copyright © 2017 Bert Bateman.

All rights reserved. No part of this book may be used or reproduced by any means, graphic, electronic, or mechanical, including photocopying, recording, taping or by any information storage retrieval system without the written permission of the author except in the case of brief quotations embodied in critical articles and reviews.

This book is a work of non-fiction. Unless otherwise noted, the author and the publisher make no explicit guarantees as to the accuracy of the information contained in this book and in some cases, names of people and places have been altered to protect their privacy.

WestBow Press books may be ordered through booksellers or by contacting:

WestBow Press
A Division of Thomas Nelson & Zondervan
1663 Liberty Drive
Bloomington, IN 47403
www.westbowpress.com
1 (866) 928-1240

Because of the dynamic nature of the Internet, any web addresses or links contained in this book may have changed since publication and may no longer be valid. The views expressed in this work are solely those of the author and do not necessarily reflect the views of the publisher, and the publisher hereby disclaims any responsibility for them.

Any people depicted in stock imagery provided by Thinkstock are models, and such images are being used for illustrative purposes only.
Certain stock imagery © Thinkstock.

ISBN: 978-1-5127-9476-2 (sc)
ISBN: 978-1-5127-9477-9 (hc)
ISBN: 978-1-5127-9475-5 (e)

Library of Congress Control Number: 2017910950

Print information available on the last page.

WestBow Press rev. date: 08/01/2017

DEDICATION

I would like to dedicate this book to my wonderful parents Clayton and Vella Bateman for the Christian training and values they tried to teach me and my brother Robert.

Robert, who is a large part of my life playing a large part in teaching and keeping me out of trouble?

My son Dean and wife Susan were very helpful. Dean helped by reading and correcting and keeping my computer running. They also gave me two wonderful grand children.

Dean is also a Baptist minister and Pastor of about fourteen years of whom I am well pleased.

My grand children and great grandchildren were the main reason for writing this. They were always encouraging me to write down some of "those good ole stories Pa Paw."

Grand children are just that "grand." I sure am proud of mine.

Shawn, our grand son, and wife Emily and their five are Missionaries to Argentina but now are in Peru studying language and the culture of South America. Those wonderful great grand children are Ian, Bethany, Carolina, Savannah, and Madelyn. They are all going to Christian School and Christian training.

Elisha "Sugar" Bateman Greene, our grand daughter, lives close by and does a wonderful job parenting two wonderful great grand children, Andrew and Ellie. She has her plate full and running over trying to home school, teach Sunday school, and work part time, and keeping the home running. She is doing a fantastic job. She also is getting in piano lessons and Christian singing. Only by the Lord's blessings would she be able to do all of this.

Both of my grand children are graduates of Tabernacle Christian College of South Carolina.

I could never express all that my family means to me.

My wife Phyllis Has always been a support and encourager in everything I do. I thank God for her and all she has contributed.

I would like to express my gratitude and love for my friends and relatives mentioned in this book. They are all part of my life that have made my life full and worth living.

I would like to express my appreciation to Jim and Faye Woods who were very helpful about the Ralph Woods store, Jim's father's store at Kyle and also the old band mill which was a big part of the community in the 1940's.

My first memories begin back sometime in 1941, probably sometime in March. The way I remember this, it was the biggest snow we mountain folk had ever seen.

My mother, Vella Bateman, bundled me up in a little snowsuit she had ordered from Sears and Roebuck, and set me out in the snow, which came up under my arms. That spring, I think it was, we got our tricycles. We had a lot of fun on them. I found the seat for mine just awhile back over behind our mailbox. The rust had taken its toll on it. I cleaned it up the best I could and sprayed it with red paint then labeled it for a keepsake. Beside a photograph, this is all the physical evidence from the time enjoying those tricycles. These are some of my first fond memories of growing up here in the mountains of Western North Carolina in the Nantahala community.

The road we lived on was paved with dirt in the summer and mud, snow, and ice in the winter. Bateman Road became almost impassable by car in the winter months. There were very few cars in those days anyway. Sometime later Bateman Road became known as Long Branch Road. Long Branch Road was on the north side of Bateman Gap and Bateman Road on the south side and also was first called Bateman Branch and Bateman Road.. When the state put up road markers, it was changed to Long Branch Road.

The Nantahala community was made up of several creeks and branches that were originally followed by trails and wagon roads. These later were improved into dirt roads passable with Model T and Model A Ford cars.

This community was served by five or six Churches which were pastored by three or four pastors who held services one or two times each month. Each pastor's finicial support was one to two dollars each when he preached. Times were hard with wages normally only ten to fifteen cents an hour a dollar was about ten hours of wages. The best things in life back then weren't purchased with money, and I think that still applies.

In this time period (and I am sure further back in time) the people were very self- sufficient. Most people lived primarily off the land. Farming began early in the spring with the plowing and preparing the field for planting. The planting was a family affair. Sometimes the children had to be kept out of school for a day or two to help with the planting

First the potatoes had to be planted, if possible in the last half of April. After this the corn must be planted which was usually around the middle of May to avoid the frosts. By then school was usually out. This was also when most of the gardens were planted.

Most families were large, with, four to ten children. When the children were old enough, they were taught to work and pitch in to help supply food and lay up food for the winter. This was the only way they could survive. The good Lord supplied abundantly also. Wild berries were something to behold. I have seen acres of old fields red with wild strawberries. Blackberries were so abundant that you could usually pick a gallon without leaving your backyard. These were really taken fast advantage of quickly. It was nothing to hear some of my friends boasting, "We have seventy cans of strawberries." Or "We have over a hundred cans of blackberries." Now, they weren't talking about quarts every time. A lot of the larger families would can food in half - gallons cans. There were also a lot of jams and jellies and various other foods stored.

I won't attempt to tell all the ways these mountain people had for survival; but I must include that every family kept at least one milk cow, two or three hogs, a flock of chickens and other farm creatures to supplemented their food and livelihood. Looking back, I sometimes wonder how we made it. God just supplied abundant grace for a hard working people of faith. Where did all of those abundant fruits come from? You can hardly find enough strawberries nowadays to get a taste. You might find enough blackberries to make a cobbler, if you have the patience to look for them.

God has been so good, and He still is. He's still supplies all of our needs.

OUR HUMBLE HOME

Our little four room house was just a little south of Bateman Gap. My Granny Elizabeth Bateman lived between us and Bateman Gap. We always called her Granny Lizzie as a lot of other people in the community also did. My Dad, Clayton, built our house. He cut the logs off of our property and Ralph Wood sawed the lumber on Long Branch and hauled it to this side of the gap to the building site. Dad split oak boards for the roofing from board trees. It took a special kind of oak tree to make good boards, I have been told.

All of this work was done with very simple tools. He used a clear bowl with a ring inside for a level. By filling the bowl with water up to the ring he could tell when it was level when the water aligned with the ring. He must have bought a hammer, handsaw and square. I can always remember that he had those. I still have the old hand crafted wood block plane he used to rough plane the lap siding weather boarding. All of the siding was American chestnut and also most all the lumber that went into the house. After all the sawing and nailing were done, my Uncle Ralph laid on two coats of white lead base paint and green on the trim. I think he did this after my Dad, Mom, and brother Robert had moved in. I think the house building was started in 1934. I was born in 1937. Dad never got the house done. Every time he had some extra money to spare he would make improvements. Later he added some side rooms on the back which consisted of a kitchen, a bedroom and a small screened porch at the upper corner. Uncle Ralph again did most of the work. This part of the building project I can remember. This probably occurred in 1942 before Uncle Ralph enlisted in the Navy. My Uncle Ralph was very close to us children. He gave Robert and me our first daisy air rifles. We sure had a lot of fun shooting those trainer guns.

EARLY SCHOOL DAYS

Now let me introduce myself. My name is Bert Bateman, the younger of two sons of Clayton and Vella Bateman. I was born July 18, 1937. My brother Robert was about three years older than I.

My mom didn't start me in school until I was about seven years old because we had to walk about two and one half miles to the Kyle School and the winters in these mountains were very harsh in the early 40's. These formative years were very rough but happy. I missed a lot of days of school due to bad weather. We had some of the deepest snows ever recorded in the early 40's. Mom had to do a lot of home schooling. Miss McCoy was my first grade teacher. She had first and second grades. Miss Roper taught third, fourth, and fifth. Lolita Dean, Principle, taught sixth seventh and eighth.

Miss McCoy sure had a lot of patience with us kids. Somehow I made it into the second grade. Robert was in the fourth grade at this time.

When I was in the first grade, Miss McCoy had a real good system about letting us children go to the outhouse. She went outside and got two short sticks and laid them on a shelf next to the door. As long as there was a stick on the shelf you didn't ask to be excused. All you had to do was to take a stick and go to the outhouse. When you came back you laid the stick back on the shelf, then some one else could go. This worked like a charm for a while until someone had the bright idea of picking up another stick or two so their buddy could go with them. Well it didn't take too long for most of the children to be outside playing around. Miss McCoy had to drop everything and go outside and herd those little rascals back into the classroom. Yes you know this ended the system "take a stick" for "May I be excused." It took a lot of patience and love to teach us children.

I don't know how or when I learned to read. I memorized what I saw below the pictures. You know, up, up went Bushy tail; up, up went Billy coon and it showed the squirrel and coon climbing up the tree. And there was the one about, play ball Mac, see Mac run. The picture showed the little dog playing and running after the ball. If you hid the pictures, I didn't have a clue what it said. Well somewhere along the way I finally caught on.

I remember walking the road to school many cold mornings. The road was so muddy sometimes that we would leave the road, especially through Kyle which was a level area, and take to the banks and fields to dodge the mud. When the mud holes were frozen over, sometimes ten to fifteen long spaces, we would skate on the ice. A lot of times this didn't have a happy ending as you can imagine.

GOING TO TOWN

At the other end of White Oak Lane that lay between Cold Spring and White Oak Creeks, we came to town as we knew it. This area of Nantahala was called Kyle, North Carolina and was town to us for many years. This community consisted of White Oak Flats Baptist Church, English Lumber Company sawmill, located up White Oak Creek about a three hundred yards.

Kyle, over time had about five stores and a post office. At the first junction was Cold Spring road the first store was about seventy-five yards up this road, some Johnson lady had a small store. Turning West on White Oak Lane, between the bridge and The Church was the Dwight Waters store. At the junction of White Oak Lane and Wayah Road was the Ralph Woods Store on the right. Later this became the Clyde and Tuny Morgan Store. Then, as you turn North down White Oak Creek, White Oak Lodge was on the left and Kyle Post Office and store, opposite the White Oak lodge. Next down the creek on the right was a water powered corn mill, called the Luther Rowland mill. This was a place we visited about every week or two to get a turn of corn ground. I don't know why we called it a turn of corn but that was what everyone called it. I always loved going to mill and getting to see Uncle Luther start that mill up and grind corn He was hopping and running up and down the ladder turning wheels and adjusting everything. He always took a toll, a small amount per bushel to pay for grinding the corn. He sure knew what he was doing.

The first thing he would do was to dump the corn into the hopper. Then he would climb those steps to the top of the large reservoir containing thousands of gallons of water. He then turned a wheel that was connected to a valve in the bottom of the tank. When he opened this it allowed the water to escape and hit the impeller blades with great force and this started the mill with all those belts and wheels turning, a sight I will never forget. What a sight for a small boy. Sometimes Luther had to run back up the ladder and readjust the speed if it got too fast. He was very careful to leave a little corn feeding into the mill as your corn finished grinding. This kept the grinding stones from coming in contact. If this happened it would get grit in the meal, which was a no, no. Everything had to be just right to make that corn into meal and Uncle Luther was a certainly a good miller. He also had a griss mill where he ground feed for livestock at one time, and he operated a dynamo to give lights for the lodge.

As you start from the junction toward the schoolhouse Bruce and Edith Duvall had a store on the left. This was where the gravel road began and as I remember this was before Clyde and Tuny had their store. As a small kid I remember navigating this road all up hill the last mile and half to school. It seemed that ever step you took that gravel would roll out from under your feet and you would roll back a half step. Then there were the big trucks to dodge, the trucks hauling logs to the band mill, and Teas Extract trucks hauling acid wood and pulp wood to Andrews where it was then loaded on train boxcars and shipped. These trucks couldn't easily slow up because most of them didn't have good brakes and they were heavy loaded. We kids had to get out of the road as far as possible and try to hold our breath until the dust settled. A few times we barley arrived at school on time due to road and weather conditions, and sometimes other distractions.

When we arrived, weather permitting, we lined up in front of the school, girls on one side and boys on the other to salute the flag. After filing into class we recited the Lord's Prayer and the teacher read scripture before taking up books. When the weather was real cold we would make a ring of seats around the pot belly stove to get warm. Sometimes this would take an hour or two. We had to wear our coats a lot of the time. During this warm up time we would read our reading assignments because we couldn't do much writing while sitting around the stove.

At one time my Granny Lizzie and some other women in the community made hot soup meals in a little two room building close by the schoolhouse. Granny made a large garden in the summer for the purpose of making soup to feed the children. I found her receipt the county paid her for this project, about twelve dollars annually. What hard working and caring people we had to help us in those trying times. That hot soup and crackers sure tasted good on those cold winter days.

A lot of the times in the early afternoons the teachers would release the older boys to go to the surrounding woods to gather kindling and wood to supplement the heating. To us boys this was a time to run the woods and play. We built wigwams and hideouts and just had a big time romping through the woods. In the spring we went a little further in the mountains and brought in mountain birch and ramps. Sometimes the wonderful aroma of ramps got some of the boy sent home.

Sometimes we would get a little bit of broken brush and pile it up ready just in case that we lost track of time and the bell rang and we wouldn't have anything to carry in and throw down to show that we had been hard at work. I don't see how we learned anything. I didn't learn very much. Most of what I learned was the good memories I have of those early school days.

I remember the bigger kids had a flying jenny. This was a crude carousel where they had rounded the top of a stump and drilled a hole in the center and fastened a sixteen foot pole with a steel rod in the center. This allowed the pole to spin around and around. This contraption must be kept in balance with the same number of kids on each end and approximately the same weight. At least two would ride while one or two would stand outside and push. This was a very dangerous play thing and must be closely supervised. Mom would not let us have anything to do with this flying jenny.

At recess or after lunch we played all kinds of games such as ball, horse shoe, and marbles. As I recall marbles was played very much because everyone got a good supply of marbles for Christmas.

Occasionally an altercation or fight would break out when one of the boys lost all his marbles. This would require the swift hand of justice from Miss Dean, a small lady but carried a big paddle. She usually held short court to try to find out who was at fault before applying the correction. Just knowing that she was close by was a great deterrent to squabbles.

Miss Dean and Miss McCoy both grew up in hard times In Burning Town Community, a little community between Franklin and Nantahala, North Carolina. Miss McCoy was Miss Dean's Aunt. They both grew up on small farms, mostly living off the land; but resolution and determination to get an education and a better life led Miss McCoy, then also Miss Dean to teaching school. I don't know how they managed their little homesteads while they were teaching. I was never at was at Miss Dean's home; but I have heard that she kept chickens, goats, ducks, pigs, a cow, and dog; all running free range where the dogs, chickens and smaller animals could come in the house to receive petting and maybe feeding. This was not unusual for life in the Appalachians in the early part of the century. I think teaching was a lot more pleasant and enjoyment in those days than it is today. The children were in general well behaved and had a close relation with the teachers.

Beside all the regular games like baseball, pitching horseshoes, marbles and others, a lot of the boys had those tepees "wigwams" nearby the schoolhouse. This was a big thing in all the mountain schools in those days. Radio story broadcasting was young. Cowboy and Indian stories just starting to hit the airwaves and at the same time taking over the minds of those little renegades and cowboys it began to show up in the games we played. Television had never been thought of back then but we could still see the Lone Ranger and Silver on mental imaginary just the same.

I finished the third grade at Kyle School and transferred to Otter Creek School the next year beginning the fourth grade.

These two schools were about six miles apart. By doing this we were able to ride the school bus from Kyle to the Otter Creed School. This cut out about three miles of walking each day. Kyle School was just an elementary school, grades one through eight. Otter Creek was an elementary and high school.

This change was altogether a new experience for me. The rules had changed. If you missed more than twenty day you couldn't pass into the next grade. That winter in the forth grade I had the flue, then complications, colds and sickness and at the end of the year I had piled up too many absences. That was what was written on my report card, too many absences, failed.

In retrospect I think it was good for me. After this I settled down and started trying to learn a little bit more.

The next year I had a wonderful teacher Mr. Ed Carpenter. Ed was good for me even though I and all the others were very naughty. Several times he would loan his new pocket knife to one of us boys to go to the lower end of the school ground to cut him some willow sprouts to whip with. I think he really just used them to scare us with. It never failed when they got back and he took one swing, he found that every one had been ringed with the knife and they flew into short pieces about twelve inches long. He usually ended up with one or two long enough to be used for a pointer.

Ed and I had a good relationship. I had received a learner's mandolin for Christmas and was trying to learn to play. Ed was a good mandolin player and he told me to bring mine to school and he would help me. Elmer May also played the mandolin and we would get together at recess and lunch and play. This was very helpful to me. In later years after Ed retired we met again. Ed was even better than when he was young. I got to play with him and his son Ben also. Ben is a very good musician. What a reunion we had! He told me that teaching at Nantahala Schools was the best years of his life.

Well I wasn't the good little boy at all times; sometimes quite the opposite. When I went to Otter Creek School I started getting to know some of my cousins and others that I think we were bad influences on one another. There still weren't too many cars in the community and sometimes when there was an event at school we had to walk. We would take a flashlight and shortcut across Otter Mountain and we could be at the school house in about forty-five minutes. By the way this was the same route that my mother and others in bygone days used to walk to school from Long Branch before school buses. This was a wagon road that was barely passable by horse and wagon and maybe by car at certain times of the year.

One cool morning my first cousin Kenneth Bateman and I decided to go on early across Otter Mountain to school.

We didn't have any preconceived plan to do mischief, but we didn't need a plan. Mischief was just part of us. We just wanted to get there early and go to the old gym and shoot some basketball and play around. Well, somewhere along the way we picked up some little demons and they took control of two little rascal minds. Upon arriving at the school house, we just walked on into our classroom to leave our lunch and things. In those days, nobody locked anything. I don't know if there was a lock on anything at the school.

"Ken do you think we ought to start a fire?" I asked.

BERT BATEMAN

"I don't know. Thay's plenty of paper." Ken responded, while stuffing the stove full.

"We still have plenty left, Ken, What are we going to do with all this paper?"

"I don't know." Ken said as he began to pull the stove pipe apart, I picked up paper and began to stuff it into the pipe. This was just a spur of he moment thing. I don't know what got into us to cause us to do such a prank. I reckon we planned to build a fire at first.

Now, this was a three-room schoolhouse with a single central flue. Each room had a stove pipe running from the pot belly stove located about ten feet in the center of the room. We did a good job stuffing that pipe full all the way over to the flue. It took all we could muster up even what we had already put in the stove to fill that long pipe. After purtying everything up, we went on to the gym and started practicing our shots. After a little while everyone began to join us saying that they had a problem over at the school house. "The whole house is full of smoke." It was at least an hour before they got the smoke cleared and the pipes cleaned out and fires built. After everything was cleared the bell rang to start classes not long before morning recess. They are still looking for the culprits (those dirty little rascals that done such a thing). There was warrant put out and reward offered for any information leading to who done it, but nothing resulted from it. Carl Moses lusted to have the ones that done this caper. No one knew who "done it". Well, if they did they sure weren't talking.

"Do you know anyone Ken? I shore don't." I asked Kenneth.

"I don't know nothing" Ken replied.

When the teachers quizzed each student as to what do you

know. "I was at the gym practicing free throws when I first heard about it." I replied.

"Kenneth, what do you know?" the teacher asked.

"I was over at the gym and somebody came and said don't go over to the school house until the bell rings. Everything is all smoked up over there." Ken said.

Until this day I don't know what got into two good boys; well we were good most of the time. What could cause them to swerve this direction? Neither one of them had any thought as to doing this. They didn't even seem to think about what they were doing it was as though it just happened. I really don't think they did it. Both of these boys had better training and upbringing. Some evil force just seemingly infected their mind for just a few short minutes. They never had done anything similar to this before or after. This one time, I reckon, was an exception.

ENGLISH LUMBER COMPANY

The band mill as everyone called it was the only public work in the community of Kyle.. In one way or another this operation provided work to fifty or more men of the community. It took about twenty men to operate the mill. There were two or three logging camps with men sawing timber and logging and log truckers hauling logs to mill. I don't know how many truckers were employed to haul and deliver lumber.

The band mill was pulled by a large steam engine. The steam was generated by a furnace and boiler that was fired with residue from the logs that were being sawed; this required one man full time to watch after the furnace. People in the community would set their clocks by the saw mill whistle. The whistle blew at 7:00 o'clock to start work, then at 12:00 noon for lunch, 1:00 o'clock back to work, and at 4:00 for quitting. This could be heard for miles around through out the community.

"What time is?" someone would ask.

"The sawmill whistle just blowed about five minutes ago." Someone would reply.

This sawmill whistle was surely an icon of those days as we were growing up in the 40's and early 50's.

Another thing the band mill had that the rest of the community was lacking was electric lights. About dusk dark the lights came on. There were lights scattered through the mill and along the roads and the camp and lobby and all the bunkhouses. I think the timekeeper and some of the others of supervision had lighted cabins. This power was produced by a small turbine and dynamo set up next to the creek with the creek supplying water to turn the turbine.

This mill was a great help to the community that wouldn't have had any other way of earning livelihoods. The pay wasn't that great and the work was hard but people in that time were used to hard work and they just appreciated a way of making a living.

My Dad was head cook most of the war years from about 1940 to 1945. Sometimes he would take the family with him on Sunday afternoons when he had to be there to prepare supper for the ones that were from Waynesville and Sylva that were special operators of the mill. These people would straggle in from 3:00 to 6:00 o'clock and he had to be there to have hot meals ready for them. Some times Mom, Robert, and I would go up there after Church and stay a couple of hours; then we would walk on home while Dad cleaned up. We always enjoyed the chance to get to explore the place and see what we could find. We had our limitations where we could go.

Above the camp there was a row of bunkhouses. These were small houses that the men could sleep in during the week days that commuted back to their homes on the weekends or lived too far in the community to walk home after a hard days work.

Robert and I like to climb the steps and run on the narrow porches and just fool around like little rascals. I haven't forgotten even till today a lesson I learned. I remember noticing a little tail sticking out between two planks on one of the cabins.

"It will be real funny to surprise that ole mouse by catching him by the tail." I thought.

The joke turned out to be on me. That ole mouse had mighty sharp teeth and a lot of fight in him to be such a small little thing. He simply turned around and took a big bite out of my finger. Lesson learned, you don't mess with a mouse's tail. I was ready to go home at that time. Robert just had a good laugh.

A few times I got to see the mill in operation. That big band saw could zip through a three foot log like it was hot butter. The operator of the carriage, Hue Wright the sawyer, I think it was, sure knew his job. It seemed he enjoyed what he was doing. It was all done in rhythm. Those boards were dropping off faster than two men could keep them moving out of the way. There was very little automation in the operation; most everything was run manually, but every man knew his job and didn't care to work.

One man kept the saw blades sharpened and repaired. Just any body couldn't do this job. It took someone trained and experienced with a lot of skill. I noticed he kept about six saw blades hanging in the shop where he worked. I was too small to remember a lot of detail about those band saw blades except they were hung up ready when they were needed. They were about six inches wide and probably made a ten-foot circle. When a blade got dull or a tooth got broken, he had to have a spare ready to replace it. That was the primary job of the saw filer but he probably filed the crosscuts and axes the timber cutters used in the logging camps plus there were a lot of other saw blades used in the mill beside the band saw blades. There were edger saws and cutoff saws that must be kept up.

Like I said this mill generated a lot of jobs and businesses. The general stores sold Work gloves, shoes, socks, overhauls, shirts, and other clothing as well as groceries and all kinds of hardware. In those days you didn't run to town every time you needed these items. There were very few cars and trucks owned by the locals and if you could drive to town, it required the better part of the day. Life was at a slower pace in those days. The roads condition limited travel to about fifteen to twenty miles per hour; and the roads wound around every hill and valley.

A lot of business men went to the White Oak Lodge from the band mill. There were always lumber buyers and salesmen looking for a place to spend the night or a few days. A lot of people just wanted to see the operation of the mill and would choose to stay overnight at the Lodge. The Company owner's wives would sometimes visit for a week. The whole community benefited from the band mill. My Dad walked most of the time to work about one and one quarter miles over the old dirt road to the mill.

I remember in the summer of 1944, on a beautiful spring Sunday morning, I was in the bedroom taking my weekly bath in a number two washtub, when I heard an airplane come over the house top. I had never heard an airplane in trouble before but I knew something was wrong with this plane. This thing began to miss and backfire something terrible. It was just circling and the popping and cracking got worse. The pilot took the plane through Bateman Gap, down Long Branch and circled back South up White

Oak Creek. He had spotted the level fields of White Oak bottoms. The saw mill was located at the upper end of this bottom land. He didn't touch down until he had crossed the White Oak Lane, just west of the old White Oak Church. The plane's left wing clipped an apple tree about two hundred feet West of white Oak Church. About three hundred feet further the plane flipped over on its back. Some of the men living near by ran to see if the pilot was ok. Upon seeing the pilot was alive, he ran back and got some tools to chop him out. After dragging the pilot out, they found him to be ok, just shaken up and bruised a little bit. He was a trainer pilot from South Carolina Air force base and traveled out too far and ran out of fuel.

Now this was one of the biggest things that ever happened in our community. I believe everybody on Nantahala heard this plane. The Lackey family, living on the north side of Bateman Gap saw and heard the commotion.

"It came right over that poplar tree above the house." Hubert said.

This brought people from all over everywhere to see what had happened. At this time of my young life I had never seen as may people at one time. Of all the people that were there, there was not a single camera in the crowd. I have never seen a single photograph of this miracle. It had to be a miracle that the pilot was unhurt.

The following week they sent a crew in with a flatbed truck and cut the plane up and hauled it away. People are still talking about the plane crash and how God helped that young trainer pilot through what could have been a tragedy that turned out to be a miracle.

ROAD WORK

Most of the side roads were kept up just for horse and wagons. Cars could navigate them in dry weather only. I remember in those days that my brother Robert and I were thrilled to hear the road grader coming up the road. I remember now all the roads in our area were just dirt roads as most of the secondary roads were that way in those days. We were just starting to recover from the depression. We would hear the road grader coming. We called it the road scraper. The State Highway Department, I guess it was called. Well, whatever it was named they managed to get over here from Franklin in the late summer just before school started and hit it twice, once coming and once going. We always liked to get behind that thing barefoot and walk on that smooth freshly graded clay dirt. I can still feel that cool feeling on the bottom of my feet. What a thrill just to watch that machine go. This was a rare treat for a couple of mountain grown little rascals. We still have those warped funny ways but I like that way and wouldn't take anything for all the wonderful memories of growing up free range in these Nantahala Mountains.

As I have said, we were just beginning to break out of the

depression as I have since read in the history books, but living at that time we didn't know anything about a depression going on. Life in these mountains was about the same before the depression, during in the depression, and after the depression. I can recall even in the 60's the Government was still trying to send educators in here to try to get us out of the depression. I think they were just making jobs for their "Carpet Baggers" buddies and wasting taxpayers' money.

Another thing that seemed to bring on a lot of talk and excitement was the convict road workers. This usually was a crew of ten or twelve convicts most of which were dressed in white and black stripe clothes.

"Did you notice?" Someone would ask "Two of those convicts had ball and chains."

"You know we don't have any locks on our doors."

They would have us kids scared to death. I remember I didn't sleep nights just thinking about that back door where there was only a latch on the screen door and one of those convicts had escaped over near the winding stairs road. They had blood hounds trying to trail them up but without any success. Word was to keep your doors locked at night.

They hauled those convicts from Franklin on the back of a truck with the truck pulling a guard trailer. The guard sat in this trailer with a double barrel shotgun. When the truck stopped the guard would get out of the trailer first and take up position then the convicts would unload. They would always have a "trustee", one that was in for some minor infraction. They would let him go around to the cold springs and get water to keep the workers cooled off. The trustee would also carry the crafts the convicts would make during bad weather such as wallets, plastic rings, etc to be sold to the public. The money would be used to buy cigarettes and other things allowed to the convicts.

We would watch the convicts through the window as they worked by our house. Mama wouldn't let us out of the house until they were well out of the way. I just wanted to see what they would do when they got to that big yellow jacket nest down there on the bank.

I didn't have to wait long until one of them made contact with those little yellow critters. You could tell he had previous experience. He jumped back off a few feet gave a few slaps and some loud words. The boss man poured a cup of oil from a can they had in the guard trailer and after the swarming yellow jackets settled, he tossed it on their nest and threw a lighted match on it. While the nest was burning, work resumed. They got a few stings but it didn't slow them down very much. They kept on swinging those bush hooks.

Kids in those days just grew up in the mountain ways and mountain lore. Certain things it seems we just knew. We were wary of dangers that always existed in the fields and woods. I don't remember being told that yellow jackets would sting you or snakes would bite or wild animals would fight if cornered. These things boys growing up in those days seemed to just know. We could tell every tree in the woods by just looking at the tree bark or the leaves. We knew what kind of twigs we could chew on; like birch, sassafras and others. We knew all the berries and edible plant fruits. Most of us could see a ginseng plant a hundred yards away. We knew where the best fishing holes were and what kind of bait to use at different seasons of the year.

Our children growing up in these mountains today don't know all of these things. Life is very much different today than it was in the 40'S. We can never return to those days.

As I have said we didn't have anything but a battery radio in the way of communication. In the summertime, it would sometimes be very hot. We had screened in windows which helped some by letting cool air in. There were a lot of people sitting out on the front porches and talk and tell stories and jokes and just talk about what happened at work or school; or what happened in their growing up years. I remember when I was about twelve years old I ripped boards and made us a porch swing. That old swing is still in storage in Dad's old truck shed. Many hot summer nights I would sit and swing. If the moon was shining I would hop on my bicycle and ride up the road to the curve and coast back down just cooling off. On Saturday nights I would swing on the porch and listen through the window to the Grand Ole Opry. I always waited until the Bill Monroe's portion came on just to hear him play the mandolin and sing. I remember the first time I heard him sing "Uncle Pen." I tried to play it on my old Sears Silvertone mandolin but my efforts came way short.

The "high lonesome sound" of his style of singing sure fit the mood of those nights. These were good old days, good old days of the 40's. Life was worth living and love was real. City folk would go insane just listening to the silence of these mountains but to us mountain people, what a thrill just listening to the night birds calling, the frogs singing, and in late summer nights the katydids chirping. This made you stop and think many times that all of this didn't evolve, as some teach, but there had to be a power greater than man to design and put it all together in harmony. Just seeing and hearing all of this should convict anyone that there is a God.

MEMORIES OF 1940'S "WWII"

On December 4, 1941, The US declared war on Germany: and on December 7, 1941 Japan bombed Pearl Harbor. I don't remember these specifically. I only remember the impact it had on me and my family and the community. Somehow my dad escaped being called for service. My Uncle Frank and later Uncle Ralph Solesbee were called. Frank served in the Army and Ralph in the Navy. Aunt Dorothy's husband, Marvin Gray also served in the Navy. At the start of the war, I was too small to remember very much. We will come back to this subject later.

A lot of things were going on in those days and news traveled slower in the mountains.

The things that stuck with me were those things that little boys do. Playing and having good times was tops of all that mattered. I discovered that I had Cousins down the road and cousins over on the other side of Bateman Gap "the Gap" we called it. The first house on the other side of the gap was where Hubert lived, a third cousin. Hubert also had two sisters Annette and Mary Lackey.

Also, my uncle Carl Bateman lived up the holler about one quarter mile on the head waters of Long Branch. Ulea, Carl's wife passed away leaving eight children Paul, Ethel, Bill, Dora lee, Eldridge, Kenneth, Betty, and Francis. It was very hard and trying on the family. Aunt Cecilia came to live with them and became a second mother in the family.

Ethel, the oldest daughter and Betty next to the youngest daughter tragically passed away, adding to the trying times.

Next down Long Branch was my Uncle Claude and Inez Solesbee with their two sons Bob and David and also Great Uncle Pat Solesbee. Then there was my uncle Ralph and Aunt Ruth Solesbee with their five children, Joan, Junior, Randy, Judy, and Jill. Jill was a late comer about the same age as my son, Dean. Next house was my grandmother's Nona Solesbee and my Uncle Frank and Aunt Dorothy lived there until Frank was drafted into the Army and Dorothy got a job working away. My Uncle Dallas built a house up on the hill where the old home place was located. This was where all of Grand paw Pinkney Solesbee's family were raised and grew up. Grand Paw Pink was tragically killed in 1939 and the family built a home closer to Long Branch on the main road. Big Granny "Nona" Uncle Frank and Aunt Dorothy lived at this house. Dallas built a new house on a driveway a short distance out the old road near where Uncle Jason and Susie Davis had lived. He and his wife Aunt Francis and their two boys Kenneth and Henry lived there.

As you go South down Bateman Road the first house on the left was Claude and Eldie Bateman. They had ten children, T.A., Geneva, Johnnie, Charles, James, Todd, Morris, Wendell, and Jerry. All of this family is our relatives, fourth cousins I think, and very close to me and our family I got on and off the school bus for many years at their home. And before that I was down at their house a lot. Morris and I went to the store about ever day in the summer months. We became very close. I think Mom sent me to the store just to give me something to do.

Most of the time I wouldn't get anything, maybe one or two items and Morris was the same. Sometimes he wouldn't get anything. He just went along with me. We had many good times playing in front of their house. Pitching horse shoe was the game we played most. Claude sat on the porch and napped. If we got too rowdy, he would open one eye

And say, "Alright hold it down boys." He never even raised his voice that I can remember.

We all liked to get together around Christmas and shoot off fire works we were never in short supply of side loaders and cherry bombs and a lot of other fireworks. It sounded like a war zone around our homes at Christmas and New Year.

During in war time everything was rationed due to the war effort. You couldn't buy anything without stamps. Gasoline was rationed but you could buy coal oil, now called kerosene. Uncle Frank would start his A Model on gas and run it on coal oil "kerosene". You could hear that A Model as soon as it crossed through Bateman Gap popping, cracking and backfiring. If you let it stop sometimes it was hard to get going again.

Dorothy wanted Frank to take her somewhere and Frank was having a terrible time getting the A Model to crank. Evidently, he had left kerosene in the carburetor.

"What's wrong with it Frankie," my Aunt asked.

"I don't rightly know. When I turn the crank, you mash the gas, that little pedal right there, and choke it a little with this lever right here under the steering wheel. Now when it hits let off the choke." Frank said.

"Turn the crank Frankie. I'll choke, strangle, or something; whatever I can do to get this thing started."

"I am about cranked out I have to rest a minute."

"Well what you reckon is wrong with it, Frankie? You think maybe it's the wheel?"

"Yea, that's what it is. The wheel won't go. We will haft to leave off going anywhere until I can get that blamed wheel to go." By this time "Frankie" was bent over the fender laughing him self to death. The A- model cranked sometime the next day when he got some gas in it.

A few days later Frank was on his way back from the CCC Camp heading back toward Kyle on his way home. After passing Kyle School, and as he approached the left-hand curve at Oscar Hicks he was distracted and just didn't make it. He went straight off into Oscar Hicks, corn field. Luckily nothing was planted in the field and he just drove out the other side. No damage was done. Only Frank's pride suffered a little. No, Aunt Dorothy wasn't with him at this time. If she had been, there might have been a lot of damage!

Not too long after Uncle Frank got his call to the armed forces and the A-model was parked in front of our old home leaning up on the side of Bateman Branch Just above where the branch runs under and across the road There it rested for about four years until Uncle Frank returned home. Then Uncle Ralph resurrected it sometime in the early fifties. But it sure did make a good place for a little boy to play and pretend to drive. I spent many good times tinkering and playing around that old car.

After a short time in boot camp Uncle Frank was shipped out to England to wait for the invasion. He didn't have to wait long, the allied forces invaded The Normandy Beach on June 6, 1944 and he was in the heat of the battle. I have heard him talk about it some but he didn't like to dwell on the subject.

As I recall he was assigned as a machine gunner to back up his buddy. If his buddy got knocked out, he had to take over. The average anyone stayed on a machine gun was about three to four minutes. His buddy took a hit in a little over three minutes and he had to take over. After he took the position he took a crossfire hit in about four minutes, entering his right front shoulder and exiting the left back shoulder. He had taken medication for such an occasion but lay there until dark, passing in and out, until the medics got him out under the cover of night and took him to back to England to an army hospital. There hadn't been time to set up field hospitals yet. He recovered fast and was back in battle in about a month. He was injured again shortly after returning to duty but this time he was injured trying to escape German artillery fire. He dived into a pit about twenty-eight feet deep and injured his leg. This caused him to be out of combat duty another stretch. He made it through all the battles until VE Day. Adolph Hitler committed suicide on April 30, and on May 7, 1945 Germany's surrender became official.

The best I can remember I was in the second grade at Kyle School, Miss McCoy told the children the good news. This was locked into my memory as though it happened yesterday.

Shortly after this, school was out for summer vacation. We were at home waiting for the boys to come home from the war. The family was very excited. Granny Solesbee, "Big Granny" we called her, came over from Long Branch carrying her sack and all she would say "Thank God he's in Franklin." As small children, we didn't know what she was talking about at first. Then she finally said someone had brought word that they had seen Frank in Franklin. It was only a few minutes later a strange car pulled up in our yard and turned and Uncle Frank jumped out. Things got pretty wild around there for awhile. There was a lot of crying, shouting and praising the Lord.

Frank thanked the man that brought him home. He later said he had started hitch hiking out of Franklin when this man pulled up and stopped and said, "Where you need to go soldier?"

"Nantahala," Frank said.

"Hop in. I'll take you where ever you need to go." The Good Samaritan said.

Back then a soldier hitch hiking was seldom passed by. People were proud of their servicemen. So in a few minutes they drove up to the house. This was the answer of many prayers.

All the boys that fought in that awful war weren't coming home. One boy in the community just down the road about one half mile, Gay Younce, the son of Eva and Preacher Harley Younce had paid the ultimate sacrifice. I remember going to his funeral just a few months earlier that was just across the highway from the Kyle School. This was a heart-breaking event for the whole community. Many similar cries went up over all the whole country for the many young men that never got to return home.

My Uncle Ralph also got to come home a little later as many other soldier boys in the community.

My Uncle Frank had received many service awards including the Purple Heart while in service. He wouldn't accept offers to rise in rank. He said he had rather just remain a private. He said the real heroes were the ones that gave all and never got to come back home. He was never the less awarded the heroes medal for valor. He lived to be about seventy-five and was buried in Arlington Cemetery in Virginia by his family, wife Kathleen, Daughter Janice, and Son Gary and their families.

THE WILD MAN HUBERT

I had seen Hubert before but that summer afternoon when I was sitting on my granny Lizzie's porch we heard a strange sound coming down the road above her house. We couldn't make out what or who it was. Just a loud rumbling, rattling noise! Then I saw something white, Hubert's cotton top flopping in the breeze as he pulled his wooden wagon along. At that time of Hubert's life his hair was almost as white as cotton. He jerked that thing to the side of the road and headed it down the short cut between the two road levels where the main road goes up and switches back and continues across the Gap. My brother Robert and I jumped up and ran over to meet him because we just knew he was going to kill his fool self. You just can't take a three foot wagon around a two foot trail on the side of a twelve foot deep ravine. Well you had to know Hubert. He at least gave it his best effort.

"Robert, hold this thing till I can get off," Hubert yelled.

He had started around that bank and the wagon just slid sideways and came to a stop and Hubert just froze, afraid to move. We held on to the wagon until Hubert dismounted. Hubert's guardian

Angel was sure working overtime in that hot July afternoon. After Hubert settled down we took the pull rope and with Hubert pulling and me and Robert pushing we rescued the wagon.

"You all right Hubert," Robert asked.

"Yea I'm alright just scuffed my heel a little. It'll be ok".

He was bare foot, and using his feet on the front axle to guide the wagon which was a very dangerous act.

He said. "You know if we had a hoe and shovel we could do a little work on this road and make a good place to ride."

"Be right back" I said. I knew granny Lizzie had the hoe and shovel.

I was back in a flash. We all three began to dig, shovel, and sling dirt and in a few minutes we had the trail around the bank plenty wide enough for the wagon to navigate safely. A few other places needed some minor work. In no time, we had a super highway constructed, always from the upper road level to the lower making a short cut.

"Help me get this thing back up there to the starting place and I'll give her a run for her money." Hubert said laughing and talking all at the same time.

He mounted up ole Dan. Dan was their horse's name. "Give me a little shove" and away he went, bouncing, jumping and hopping. He made it across the bank and headed down the steepest part. At the lower end of the steep incline there was a dog leg, we called it, and on the other side of the dog leg was a weed and sage patch. Hubert didn't quite get it straightened up and that was where he landed. There was no damage but as he got up he began slapping and beating his hair while running. "Thar's a big yellow jacket nest over in thar some wheres."

Now Ole Dan didn't have any brakes as yet. It's a wonder he made it off that hill at all.

I don't remember if he had any stings from those yellow jackets. The next day Robert and Hubert decided they would "whoop that ole jacket nest out." They both cut some good sprouts about three and half feet long with a lot of leaves. After locating where the nest was, Robert told Hubert, "I'll take the first lick and you follow with the second and we will alternate so that way the jackets can't get out."

"Sounds like a wiener to me" Hubert replied.

"Here goes," yelled Robert. It looked like a wind mill there for about a minute. Then I saw Hubert slap at that cotton top and I knew that one had got through their defense It was all over, the jackets had won round one. The next yellow jacket offensive was to burn them out. This would wait until the next day. Meanwhile the highway department had closed down the wagon road due to hazardous conditions. Also, the wagon had to be re-engineered with a guiding system and brakes. It just wasn't safe in the present condition. We added a lever and connecting rod out of wood tied on to the front axle to make it safer to guide, without having to use your feet. On the left side, we added a lever and braking system similar to a horse drawn wagon, except on a smaller scale. I don't remember which of the three engineers had this bright idea but it sure worked great and probably saved lives.

The next day was very productive in getting rid of those pesky jackets. A couple of catalogs, a long pole, strings and matches annihilated most of the jackets. And the highway department lifted the safety ban on the wagon road. Ole Dan was ready to ride again.

This also opened up a new shortcut for pedestrians which they seemed to appreciate very much. All the pedestrians used this route for many years cutting the time at least four minutes of going up and around the curve.

This four-wheel wagon just wasn't long enough for more than two passengers. So the engineering department began plans on a longer six wheeler wagon. This of course would require all new parts: one new six foot by sixteen-inch-wide by one inch thick board, preferably solid oak, an item not easy to come by. Also, three yellow locust axles and six new black gum wheels were the main requirements and this did not include braking and steering materials. I already knew where a black gum tree was that we could get the wheels from.

I can't remember how long we worked on this stretched out limousine but it took several days for everything to come together. We had to borrow Uncle Carl Bateman's auger to bore the wheels. After about a month this machine rolled off the assembly line. Boy, was she a beauty. Three or four piled on and experienced the thrill of a lifetime riding a homemade all wooden-wagon.

"All aboard?" Hubert hollered.

I was seated behind Hubert and Kenneth was behind me. I can't remember who was behind Ken. I think three riders were about all that could get on. Sometimes another rider would stand up on the back and hold on to the shoulders of the one in front of him and if the brakes started smoking too much he had the option of bailing off. Hubert let off the brake and away we went on her maiden run.

We took it easy for the first few rides. "I'm just breaking her in." Hubert said. "Boy them brakes sure makes it a lot easier to handle."

You never put grease on those axles, just a little tallow when new. After a few runs that axle was like glass and grease was never needed. We alternated at driving so we all got some experience. Those that I can remember playing and riding were Hubert, Robert, myself, Bert, Eldridge, Kenneth, and Colin, Jim, and Jack Solesbee that had moved back to Long Branch. Colin, Jim and Jack were Hubert's first cousins. They moved back in Doc Solesbee's house just below Uncle Claude's place. I can't recall the date they moved back. There were others, Junior and Kenneth Solesbee and maybe others that got their thrills riding "Ole Dan" The sequences and dates of these stories I can't always remember correctly but the good times are all locked in. I will never forget them. Sometimes I can still smell the smoke coming off the brakes when we were coming down that hill fully loaded.

I can't remember any one ever getting seriously hurt riding the wagon. Just one incident comes to mind, as I recall Hubert was driving and I was a passenger when the controls or something malfunctioned on the steep incline just before the dogleg curve. We almost flipped and Hubert slid off hitting his tail bone on something that started him to moaning rolling and screaming like a painter. "I've busted my a_ _." He screamed.

The tie rod to the front axle had come loose letting the front wheel's flip under the floor board. Hubert went home but he was back the next day. "I never told anybody." He said laughing.

I don't know how they kept from noticing the limp. This didn't slow wagon riding down very much. Everything was soon back to normal.

We could hear Hubert coming through Bateman Gap every morning about 9:00 o'clock, doing his famous train whistle by cupping his hands together and blowing across his thumb. This was a routine sound through the summer while Mom, Robert, and I were having breakfast. Mom let us sleep late after Dad had gone into work down at the sawmill. He had to leave before daylight to cook breakfast and have it in the lobby by 6:30 or before. The startup whistle blew at 7:00.

"Hubert, have you had breakfast?" Mom would ask.

"'Had two bites of egg and a bite of biscuit." He replied.

"Well, I think we have some oatmeal left and there's some blackberry jelly and biscuits "Have some if you would like" Mom said.

"I think I will. I'm getting a little bit hungry now." Hubert said as he emptied the sugar bowl into the left-over oatmeal.

After finishing off the oatmeal, he said, "I think I'll try some of that blackberry jelly."

This was a usual start of the day. We enjoyed having Hubert eat with us. There was never a dull moment throughout the day. It seems that things just happened. We played marbles in the road. We played dip up ball in the road. We never worried about cars. Uncle Claude Solesbee had the only car that ever came up the road. We could hear him coming home from working at the band mill about 5:00 o'clock.

"Well, I guess I had better be getting over the hill." Hubert would say as he headed up the road. Hubert really had an ear for that truck. I think he heard it when it left the sawmill.

Uncle Claude would always stop and pick him up. In about fifteen minutes Hubert would sometimes be back.

"I forgot my coat." was his favorite excuse.

We were always glad that he came back. Play usually resumed right where we left off. Hubert was a good horseshoe pitcher and that was one of our favorite games. All of the neighborhood kids had a horseshoe pitching place. We didn't have games to play that kids play today. We had no TV to watch. Electric power came to our community in 1946. We burned oil lamps before then. Many times I remember going to Granny Lizzie's to borrow a quart of oil so we could light the lamp for the night. We had run out of oil. For news and some entertainment, we had a battery powered radio. We listened to the Lone Ranger and Sergeant Preston and on Saturday night The Grand Ole Opera; but in summer reception was very poor on the old Philco AM radio due to thunder storms. We learned to improvise with our own entertainment. Sometimes we would just listen to the elders tell stories about their days of growing up. Believe me some of those stories were good and some were very funny and probably more entertaining than watching TV today.

Sometimes we would play checkers of fox and geese on home drawn boards. We would saw checker buttons from old broom handles and use black shoe polish to color half of them. Hubert even got pretty good at checkers This kind of games we played when it was too rainy or snowy to get outside. We enjoyed physical games most that required running jumping and roaming around in the woods.

Then Eldridge and Kenneth got a monopoly game which we all enjoyed very much. This was all new to us and time just flew by. Sometimes we would be up at their house until 11:00 O'clock at night trying to finish out a game.

FIREWORKS FOR CHRISTMAS

We were all poor by today's standards but we didn't realize our condition because everybody was poor. If we had food to eat, clothes to wear, and shelter we were "walking in high cotton."

It was a tradition to shoot off fireworks at Christmas Eve and New Years. We received other things for Christmas but we always had our share of fireworks. From two weeks before Christmas until after New Years it sounded like a range war here around Bateman Road. I wonder how our Moms stood it.

On Christmas Eve just about dark we would head to Long Branch to serenade. We always took along plenty of firecrackers to let everyone know we were coming. We would end up at Uncle Ralph's where we would always get treats and join in games with Joann and Junior our cousins playing and frolicking until we were near exhaustion. There was a long hall running the full length of their house. This was where we played blindfold. Now Uncle Ralph enjoyed the fireworks also. Sometimes he would set off some dynamite. He followed mining work and he would bring home some dynamite in case he needed to blow a stump or something out of the ground. At Christmas or holidays he would set off a stick or two to celebrate. A big bang was considered as "cool" in those days.

We dried wild animal hides and sold them to John Wishon's store. Opossum hides brought about fifty cents and gray fox hides brought about a dollar and half, and coon hides about the same. One time ole Dempsey treed and we didn't have any oil in the lantern and no flashlights. He barked and persisted so long that Mom finally said we will take the lamp and go to him. He was above the road and back on this side of the Gap. Finally we made our way up to where he was and spotted the possum up in a small white oak. I don't know how she got the sights lined up by that lamplight but that possum tumbling out on the first shot with that 22 rifle. We didn't question was it worth the fifty-cents that we would get for the hide. What we were trying to do was to stop ole Dempsey from barking all night. He was a real good watch dog. I have wondered if that dog was named after Jack Dempsey the champion boxer. Every family had at least one dog on the farm to watch about wild varmints catching the chickens and pigs and small animals. A good watch dog would always sound the alarm if any prowlers came around.

As for putting meat on the table most all of our dogs would tree squirrels, rabbits, coons, and groundhogs but we didn't depend too much on these for food. We did eat a lot of squirrels. I remember of having one groundhog that Robert and Hubert caught in a steel trap. This groundhog was not full grown. We dressed it and mom cooked, and baked it. It was very good. At least we thought it was.

I didn't get much more than a taste. Robert and Hubert gobbled it all down before I could the second bite.

I think, what we enjoyed most with the dogs was getting into the woods and hunting. Least ways that's what we called it; but it was mostly just romping and exploring the mountains, having fun, free ranging the hills, and growing into little hillbilly rascals.

We didn't get much book learning but we weren't lacking in mountain lore and how to survive in hard times living in these mountains. We learned all the edible herbs and also things to stay away from. We knew all the poison plants like poison ivy. poison sumac and others. We also could identify ginseng, May apple plant, lady slipper, black snake root, catnip plants, and other medicinal plants. We could identify most all trees either by the bark or leaves.

My Dad taught me to bud and graft apple and fruit trees at a very young age. I had better luck back then than I do now.

These things most children growing up in our present time just don't learn. It's a different time and different means of making a living. Modern technology has taken over. Computers have replaced books. Calculators have replaced mathematical knowledge.

In growing up in the forties we were much more down to earth. We were geared a different way; a lower gear and much closer to earth and reality. Sometimes I wonder if this modern way of live is better. It seems we are forced into it and there is no way to avoid it.

Would we really want to return to the "good old days?" I really don't know if we could even if we wanted to.

Only God knows the future. Only He can safely take us there!

It is good to wander back through our memories to those wonderful days of growing up in these mountains. I know our son, Dean, has memories of the sixties and early seventies. Our grandchildren Shawn and Elisha will have great memories of the eighties and my grandchildren Andrew and Ellie Greene and Shawn and Emily's five Ian, Bethany Caroline, Savannah, and Madelyn now living in Peru on Missionary training but really enjoy getting to visit the mountains when they can. I hope they will all have some memories of the mountains

I hope this will give them all a glimpse back to the days of my childhood of 1937 to 1957 that we was roamed and free ranged these hills. This was a time of great change and growth for the country and community, the hard, the good and beautiful times.

FIRST SWIMMING HOLE

The three little mountain rascals engineered and built our first swimming pool, if you could call it that. Hubert, Robert and myself were out just fooling around down in the laurel thicket about one hundred yards down the road below the house. I can't recall any planning or anything relating to this project. Maybe we got the idea from the one that our first cousins Cecil, Herbert and Ted had built further down the branch It just seems that things just happened when we were out roaming around. Anyhow we ended up in the branch. This branch was called Bateman branch back in those days. Later I found out that it had been called Camp Branch. There are many Camp Branches around. This branch had its head in our old Pasture a couple hundred feet up past our barn. We pulled our shoes off and rolled up our pant legs and just began splashing around in the water. I don't know who thought of damning the water. I reckon it was Robert. We started moving the rocks to a place where the branch narrowed.

"Come and help me with this one, Robert." Hubert hollered. "It's so big that I can't budge it."

That happened more than once as the construction proceeded.

I pulled up weeds and grass tussocks and anything to help stop the water.

"I'm getting my pants wet." Hubert laughed. "I think I'll just pull them off."

So off came everybody's pants and shirts too.

Robert was standing at the lower end next to the dam ."Look." He said. "It's getting deep. It's already above my knees."

"Here, take this turf and stop that leak over there, Robert. Just a little more and she will be ready." Hubert said, giggling with excitement all the time.

"Well," without warning, "here goes," He yelled as he sprawled out in the water splashing and thrashing. He took me by surprise and splashed water all over me. The water was cold too.

Then we all three hit it. Just splashing and hollering. This was our first swimming lesson.

After Hubert thrashed and splashed for awhile, he climbed out. "I am just about to swim. I think if I put my pants on is all I'll need." Hubert said. In three jerks of a sheep's tail he jerked his pants off that laurel bush and was back in, splashing and kick all over the pond with his pants on.

"Does that help any, Hubert?" Robert asked.

"Yea, some but I need a little more." He said, as he climbed out again.

"Where's my shirt?" He pulled his shirt on and back into the water he went. This time he did a belly splat. It sounded like a boat paddle hit the water. After splashing around for several more minutes, we heard mom holler and we knew dinner was about ready.

"We're coming," Robert answered.

We all climbed out and put our clothes on. Hubert just had to put his shoes on He already had his clothes on, soaking wet.

When we got up to the house mom gave Hubert some of Robert's clothes to put on. They were a little too big but they were dry.

"It'll be a little while before dinner will be ready. I'm running a little behind." Mom said. "If I had a little help, it would be ready quicker."

"What are you having?" Hubert asked.

"Pinto beans, fried potatoes, corn on the cob, corn bread and I'm stirring up a blackberry cobbler." Mom said.

"Yummy, yum---yum, I love pintos. The more you eat the better you feel. Eat pinto beans every meal. What do you want me to do?" Hubert laughed and said.

"For one thing, the dining table needs clearing. Take this dish towel and get all the breakfast crumbs off. Then dampen it up a little and wipe it off." She instructed Hubert. I think she just wanted to keep us busy.

Meanwhile that little demon began whispering in my ear. Hubert had left the dish cloth lying on the corner of the table while he was carrying some crumbs off. That little demon said get the mouse trap and set it under that towel. Ok, sounds good to me. That won't hurt him, just scare the stuff out of him. I had to move fast to get out of there before he got back. I just made it in time to get everything set up and run out the front door and get to back of the house where I could peep through the window to watch the action.

Hubert came back through whistling and skipping high. He was really having fun doing KP and I believe he was hungry after nearly learning to swim. That had taken a lot out of him. He might have had blackberry cobbler haints kicking around under that cotton top too.

Bang! "Oh….Oh." Hubert cried. "My finger is broke" as that mouse trap and dish towel flew across the room.

Me and that little demon ran off out in the yard and lay down and rolled and laughed.

"That's done it. I'm getting out of here". Hubert ran out the door holding his finger moaning.

Mom came to the door and said, "It's ready, come on, I'm putting it on the table."

It was a wonderful sight to behold the healing power for Hubert's finger those words had. I never heard another word about the broke finger again. I don't remember Hubert doing anymore KP from that day forward.

LEARNING THE GRAPEVINE ROPES

My dad, Clayton, was doing some plowing on the Campbell Mountain; this mountain was named after a family that lived up there long ago. Dad had cleared up about an acre of new ground up on the side of the mountain to plant some corn and beans. Back then we didn't have money to buy a lot of fertilizer so we would plow and plant in new ground where the soil was rich. So Robert, Hubert, and I were up there fooling around where the skid road led into the field. We were just fooling around killing time on some grape vines. These were huge vines climbing from the ground all the way to the tree tops. They swung loose at the bottom and you could get in those vines and swing from one to the other. I guess we were trying to play monkey or ape or something. I don't even know if we knew what we were doing. We all had our shirts off and Hubert was placing his hand in his arm pit and flapping his arm up and down making obscene noises and laughing.

"Sounds just like ole Dan." Hubert said.

Ole Dan was Hubert's family horse.

Now I didn't see any poison ivy but I didn't look for any because it didn't poison me anyway. Later I checked it out and there was poison ivy everywhere.

Next morning Hubert's freight train came blowing through the Gap about nine o'clock. He was dressed loose with a thin shirt, unbuttoned.

"I'm eat up." He explained. "I've got poison oak all over me from head to foot."

I noticed he was holding his arms out like he wanted to fly. "You got it under your arms?" I asked.

"Yeah right." He smirked. "That's where it's the worst." Pulling his shirt back to show where Maw had painted it white with something. Hubert was in recovery mode and we didn't see him much for about a week. After that we were watchful and very careful to help Hubert avoid poison ivy.

Later on that fall we did have more encounters with grapevine swings. What little experience we had on Campbell Mountain just seemed to whet our appetite for grapevine swings. Up on the ridge on the East side of Bateman gap, up about a hundred feet or so we found what seemed a good prospect. This beautiful grapevine was about two inches in diameter secured in the top of an oak about fifteen inches in diameter and about fifty feet high. We worked a good while cutting it loose at the ground then we all three took hold and jumped about to test if it was secure. We all agreed that it was all "A" OK. There was only one quirk about this swing. It was grown close to the tree. This was no problem

if you swung on an arc around the tree. You couldn't just swing straight out and straight back as would normally be the case. You had to swing wide starting on one side and swing around the tree landing on the other side and then return the same way. We had a real good time swinging for about an hour or so everything went smooth.

Then Hubert said, "I'm going to see how fur out I can go." And he backed up on the ridge as far as he could and took a run and go full speed ahead. And he went where no man had gone before. He went beyond the point of no return. Or was it beyond the point of no turn. I reckon he just got excited and forgot to swing in an arc. He went too straight out I mean away out. Hubert saw that he had messed up and began to scream but it didn't seem to do any good, He was coming straight back toward that tree with his back facing the tree. I just closed my eyes and covered my face. I heard the impact but didn't see it. It shook that whole tree. I think some of the leaves fell off. I just knew Hubert was kilt. I think he was temporarily out. I felt better when I heard him screaming.

"Oh my head I've busted my head wide open. Robert, look up there and see if my head is busted. Oh my head I'm messing all over myself. I'm going to the house and tell Maw. I'll get the axe and cut that old grapevine down. Robert, look up thar and see if my head ain't busted."

"No, all I see is a big pump knot on the back side. I believe you will be alright in a few minutes." Robert said trying best as he could to comfort him.

Hubert was tough. He was mountain grown and a red necked little rascal if I have ever seen one. He wallowed around and moaned for awhile then he was ready to go. We went on around the mountain to see what else we could get into. I can't remember ever going back and swinging on that same grapevine again. Although we did have other swings later on.

Talking about how tough Hubert was, reminds me of one event that I still find hard to believe. We all went barefoot a lot of the time from early spring until late fall. We were all up on the mountain hunting for chestnuts. This was before disease wiped out all the native chestnuts. We found a tree that still had some chestnuts where the burrs had fallen off. Hubert started stomping those burrs with the heel of his barefoot. Yes barefoot...

"Don't them burrs stick you, Hubbie?" I asked.

"No, can't feel a thing." Hubbie said as he turned his foot up. The bottom of his feet had nature's shoe soles about a quarter inch thick that looked like leather.

Believe me Hubert was a tough mountain grown little rascal. He proved that in more ways than I can remember.

Another time when we were all playing around up at Uncle Carl Bateman's, Eldridge, Kenneth, Robert, and I, and Hubert were playing with a huge tractor tire, just rolling it around in the yard. Now this yard was a level place below the house about twelve feet wide with a rock wall at the lower side. This area ran a little more than the length of the house. All of this had been done by Uncle Carl before building his house. I don't know where that tractor tire came from.

"Eldridge, if you and Robert will pull this thing open to where I can get inside it, I'll let youns roll me around here in this level spot if youns will promise to hold on to this thing and not let me loose." You could feel the excitement building in Hubert's voice.

"Oh, we won't let you loose." Everybody agreed.

Eldridge on one side and Robert on the other pulled that tire open and Hubert slid down on the inside.

As they began to roll Hubby around slowly at first, Hubert was hollering and crying joyfully as he enjoyed the ride. And then something went awry. That tire somehow slipped out of their hands and they lost it. In a wink of the eye it went over that rock wall and went airborne jumping about ten feet high as it bounded off the bank and onto the road below that led from their house on down the branch to the main road. The further it went the faster it got, bouncing and jumping all the time. It was out of balance with Hubby inside on one side. Every time he would come to the top side that thing would leap higher. I just knew he was kilt. After a short distance, it left the road and got in the branch. When it got in the branch with all the briars and weeds it slowed and came to a stop over against one side of the branch. Everybody ran to see if Hubby was still alive.

"Help, help, get me out of here!" Hubert screamed.

He's still alive. I thought to myself. Thank God, this is a miracle.

They pulled the tire open and Hubert climbed out slowly and hit the road running.

"I'm going to the house." He snubbed as he went out of sight toward home. "I'm going to tell Maw."

Nobody saw Hubert for several days. Miraculously He wasn't hurt. This was just another demonstration of how tough Hubert was.

They sure don't grow them like that now days.

JUST HORSING AROUND

We liked to play ole horse, as kids growing up in the Appalachians; we were around horses a lot. A horse was almost a necessity on the farm. The horse was used to plow the fields and gardens in the spring. In the fall, it was used to help gather in the harvest. The winter heating wood had to be gathered in. The horse sure was handy in doing these chores. No wonder that children liked to play "ole horse." In the summer when the heat got to be unbearable we would strip down to our under-ware briefs and play ole horse.

Hubert would say. "Let's go to the barn lot and play ole horse."

Away we would run and crawl through the fence to play ole horse in the barn lot. No animals were in the lot in the summer, just maybe a few chickens. We would leave our clothes hanging on the fence. We would try to act like a horse neighing, kicking, pretending to pick grass, and all of the antics we had seen the horse doing. I think we even picked some sweet clover. I think Hubert was the best horse. It was dangerous to come up behind him while he was picking grass. He would rear up on his front and kick and squeal. He almost kicked me in the side of the head a few times. I started watching out for that kicking horse. I think Hubert thought he was a horse. We would keep up horse play for hours at a time, until we tired out then we were on to some other game. We will tell more about playing ole horse later.

There was a small branch running through the barn lot. Sometimes we would end up playing in this branch. One time I recall us building a pond in this branch. We picked up a hoe somewhere and we began digging off the sides of the branch and using it as building material to dam the water. We reinforced it with rocks and anything we could find. In a short time we had a large pond eight to ten feet long. Then those little demons began to work, I can't remember who of the three took the demonic message. Anyhow we all went to the barn loft and got hay seeds and trash and coated the pond over. Then I went to the crib, where we kept some corn and other feed and brought some corn. We shelled corn and scattered it around the pond and on top of the trash in the pond. After this we called the chickens. We began to throw out more corn on the pond. These big fat hens could not swim or walk on water either. They tried to fly but had a problem getting anything under wing but water. These weren't ducks. They were chickens. All those poor ole chickens could do was to tread water and thrash. It seems they kicked about all the water out of that pond while three boys laughed, rolled and hollered and rolled around on the ground.

"OLD CROW"

The first pet crow we had was when I was too small to go with the bigger boys into the woods and rob the crow's nest of the little ones. My brother, Robert and my two first cousins, Cecil and Herbert Bateman found the nest and Cecil said, "Herb get on up there and get them crows."

Herb said "I ain't doing it. If you want them crows you go right ahead."

Well, guess who climbed the tree. Cecil wanted them crows. When he got up to the nest, he took off his shirt and wrapped two of the small birds and made his way back down the tree.

You must get these birds before they get too big. When they get big enough to fly sometimes they will fly out of the nest and you can't catch them. We had this to happen once or twice. These black birds eat almost anything but we didn't know it at first. We dug night crawlers, hunted spring lizards (salamanders), crickets, grasshoppers, bugs and other insects. You could not fill that disposal. After two or three weeks "ole crow" would be taking his maiden flight. "Ole crow was the name of every crow we had and I can't remember how many we had. That is what we always named them. After ole crow started flying he was everywhere you were when you went outside. He was always a lot of fun but sometimes he could be a pesky bird and you may want to kill him.

One such incident on Sunday morning, Decoration Day at the cemetery, a lady of the community came walking down the road carrying a big box of flowers. She was walking because that was about the only mode of transportation in those days. All the ladies wore hats in those days. The ones that had the little black veils in front that came down below the eyes. Ole Devil crow had done and spied her and took up his perch on the corner fence post of the garden next to the road. As the lady sashayed by in her black dress and hat that had a beautiful red rose attached. After passing beyond the sight of the crow, ole devil crow took sail. I think he had his torpedo sight on that rose. He knocked the poor lady's hat half off her head. There wasn't anything any one could do. She shot a look that could have killed any crow or buzzard but that didn't help. Ole crow landed on the wood shed on the other side of the road waiting for the next attack. I am glad the lady had her hat pinned on. She adjusted it with one hand the best she could and gaining her composure continued down the road. Oh no, here comes the black dive bomber again. Like I said I am glad she had that six-inch hat pin through that hat and running through that neat bun that was covered. That pin is all that saved her hat from going to the ground. I had to leave the scene. I was truly sorry for the lady but I just couldn't hold back any longer.

This was just one of many devilish tricks "Ole Crow" did. There's no wonder that ole crow had such a short life, rarely making it to the second year. They didn't take to strangers very well. That was people, dogs, cats, hawks, or other crows. I remember only one thing that could put "Ole Crow on the run and that was the tiny hummingbird. Many times, Ole crow would come swooping in with a hummer in hot pursuit about a couple of inches from the back of his head. Crows have a great fear of hummingbirds.

In the summertime, we played a lot of different games outside sometimes we played over at Hubert's house, sometimes over at Elbridge and Kenneth's house and sometimes at our house. At all three places, we had horseshoe. We all got pretty good at pitching horseshoe. This was one game we all loved. I remember pitching horseshoe in the afternoons until it got so dark I couldn't see the stob. We called the stakes stobs as kids. I can never recall any fights in all the games we played. Oh, sometimes we disagreed on whose shoe was closer to the stob. That was easy to settle. We kept a measuring stick lying around and we would simply measure to see which was closer.

When we were playing in front of our house, many times Hubert would out of the blue say, "Well, it's about time I'd better be getting over the hill."

We didn't know what had happened to bring that about so suddenly and we would beg him to stay.

"Can't you stay just to finish this game? Hubey."

"Nope. If I stay too long Momma won't let me come back."

He wouldn't take twenty paces up the road until we would hear Uncle Claude Solesbee coming up the road in his truck, getting in from work down at the saw mill.

Pulling to a stop, Claude would say. "You need a ride Hubert."

"Yea, I guess so." as he climbed into the back.

Chances were that Hubert would be back in a few minutes. "'Forgot my coat. Momma said I could stay thirty more minutes."

We were always glad that he came back. Sometimes those thirty minutes would turn into an hour and thirty minutes.

Many times Ole Crow was right there trying to help whatever we were doing. If we were pitching horseshoe or playing marbles or whatever, ole crow was trying to get into the game. If he started trying to pick up the horseshoes, we would have to stop the game until he got out of the way.

We got a lot of marbles at Christmas. It seems that marbles was the favorite gift that would be given at Christmas. We would draw names at school, and guess what I got. Two out of three times I would receive a big bag of marbles. Of course, I wasn't the only one to receive marbles. You have never seen so many marbles. People didn't have much money in those days as I now realize and marbles were cheap.

One of the games we played with our marbles in the road where the rain had washed in sand giving us a smooth place to roll our marbles was "marble bowling." We would draw two lines about ten feet apart and we would line all our marbles up on the line. Each kid would line up his marbles in a space about a foot long, ten or twelve marbles. The next kid would skip a space and line up his the same. All the marbles must be touching one another. The point of the game was to take your aggie, that big marble about three times bigger than a standard marble, and while standing back at the other mark, about ten feet away roll your aggie and knock as many of you opponent's marbles as you could off line. The ones you knocked off you got to keep. Usually at the end of the game you would have about the same number of marbles as you started out the game with. That is if Ole Crow didn't take his share out of your line. This was one game ole crow could play. And, he was very good at it. He could swoop down from that cherry tree, his favorite perch where he liked to hide and wait his turn, to scoop up five or six marbles and be gone faster than old Santa Clause went up the chimney. Most the times he would carry the marbles across the road to the hillside and hide them under leaves or anything he could. Then he would rush back to get in on the game. If you tried to run him off, it just made the game more exciting for him. He would just fuzz up his feathers and calk and squawk. This was ole crow's game. He just loved those brightly colored marbles. He could break you up if he hit you two times in a row. The only way you could have beaten him at this game would be to shoot him. He was good at most anything that was mischievous. Sometimes he carried those marbles up on the roof of the old house and try to hide them under the loose boards. When it would dislodge, and start to roll off the roof, Ole crow would turn loose everything he had to try to catch that marble before it hit the ground. Ole crow certainly was hilarious.

Ole tom, our big tom cat just could not compete with Ole crow. He would slip up behind Ole tom and grab him by the tail. Ole tom would let out a squall and try to put him away with those long sweeping claws but Ole crow was just too fast. He was always gone before Ole tom could make his turn around. Against a young crow he might have succeeded but an Ole crow, no. He didn't stand a chance.

Ole Crow did have one thing going in his favor. You didn't have worry about hawks catching the chickens while Ole Crow was on guard. Hawks or any other large birds never got by Ole Crow's radar. Ole crow was always on guard ready to make that dive bomber attack. He always attacked from above. He never came up from the bottom or the front. He would gain the advantage by gaining altitude and striking from a power dive. I don't think he could hurt the hawk but he just intimidated Mr. Hawk and embarrassed him into leaving. Sorry, Mr. Hawk no chicken dinner today! I watched Ole Crow run a hawk down to Kyle and away up on White Oak creek. So far away they just looked two specks. I would hold out my arm out and wave. Old Crow would cut away and that speck in the sky would head my direction. In about two or three minutes He would land on my shoulder with that familiar "coo, caw" crow talk in my ear. Ole Crow what a beautiful and wonderful pet and friend that you are. I will never forget you Ole crow.

CORN COB WARS

I remember another one of our favorite games was corn cob fights. The biggest one of these wars games that I can remember was over at Eldridge and Kenneth's. They had a big barn and they used a lot of corn. They fed corn to hogs, horse, cows, chickens, and also to make meal for household use. Now if you were brought up on a farm you would know these cobs just accumulated every where. About all you had to do was look down anywhere around the barn, in the barn, and around all the out buildings, there would be corn cobs. Now some of these corn cobs laying in the barn lot or the hog pens could become pretty heavy and sometimes very nasty. We didn't use the nasty ones unless we got into a desperate situation. And that did happen sometimes. You know war is not good and you must resort to drastic measurements.

Now as I recall we didn't choose up and have sides it was every man for him self. You had just better watch out because you never knew who might launch the next U- F- O from some hidden hole in the wall or some unexpected corner. Now you know one of those heavy soggy ones landing on the right spot could just about take you out. And all the sympathy you got was everyone laughing and hurrahing you.

Never ever over expose yourself. Standing in an open door or in the barn loft where the hay was taken up at the front That was just like a squirrel sitting on a stump in front of a hunter with a double barrel shotguns.

I recall Hubert was just stand by the outhouse with nobody in sight when out of nowhere one of those flying objects scored him right above the eye. He came around in a little while but he wasn't able to return to action the rest of the evening.

"That was not a corn cob." Hubey said, "That was a rock or something."

Anyhow Hubert had to be taken out of action for the rest of the evening. This was a rough game. One time I received a direct hit to the eye and it cut my eye or something got in my eye and it bothered me for a day or two. It's a miracle that we didn't get seriously injured.

One of our weekend wars carried over into the following Monday evening. Eldridge was in the barn loft throwing out hay when Kenneth came around the corner and just couldn't resist such a good target. Maybe it was one of them "little demons" that came along and made him do it. There laid that big soggy corn cob and he picked it up and without thinking launched it right at Eldridge's blind side. He didn't know what hit him.

He just rolled out of that loft. If it hadn't been for that pile of hay it might have been a lot worse.

The next day he came down with the Mumps and he had to stay in bed for three days.

Those corn cob war games were rough and dangerous. Someone always ended up getting a pump-knot on the side of the head or bruised up in other ways; but never nothing very serious. I know now that those Guardian Angels were working overtime a lot of times.

Swinging in the pines

There was always a large pine thicket in our pasture. Sometimes on Sunday evenings after Church we would be playing around just scouting and free ranging hunting something to do. And we sometimes ended up playing in the pines. Sometimes we would play hide and seek, and sometimes Lone Ranger and outlaws. And sometimes we would just climb those pines and see how far we could go swinging from one tree to the other. The point was to go all the way across to the other side. The first to reach the other side won. This may not sound like such a good game. But to these little mountain rascals it was a lot of fun and exercise. It also made us tough. At the end of the day we would have a lot scrapes, scratches, maybe a few bruises, and smelling like pine but we slept real good that night.

Sometimes we would find Indian artifacts while we were roaming and playing around in the old fields. In bygone days, the Cherokee Indians lived here. Our collection was mainly arrowheads and spearheads but sometimes and more rare axes and pipes were found. Many people hunted these for sale but we never sold ours. We considered them sacred keepsakes. In our old garden spot, just above our house there was a huge flint rock that appeared to be chipped. I always believed that the Indians made their arrowheads from this stone. I found several incomplete and imperfect arrowheads in the garden.

It sure would have been good to have known more about these wonderful people that lived off the land in the olden days of these mountains. Oh well I think our God knows and has a plan. I am thankful to be a part of his great Master plan.

RAINY DAY HORSE PLAYING IN THE BARN

Hubert, Robert, and I were playing around in the road in front of the old home place. The road was about the only place we had to play that was handy. We played marbles, pass the ball, played dip up ball, red rover, pretty girl station, we had to usually substitute boys for girls in this game because we seldom had any girls to play the part. This time as I recall we were playing dip up ball. To play dip up ball we used a flat board about two feet long and some kind of a soft ball, one that had some bounce in it. The pitcher stood about twelve feet away and just pitched the ball so the batter could hit the ball up in the air. The ball must stay in the road. If you hit the ball out of the road and out in the weeds, it went out of bounds and it was a foul strike, or if you missed the ball it was a strike. When you got three strikes you had to let the next one in line take a turn. When we had enough players, we would run the bases. This was just one of our games we played to pass time and have something to do.

We had been playing sometime one Saturday in the spring when Hubert said, "Listen what was that I heard."

We all stopped briefly to listen up.

"I don't hear nuthin." I said.

Robert said, "I don't either, what did you hear, Hubert?"

"I thought it was thunder, but I guess it wussen't. Put her in here Robert." Hubert said as we started playing ball again.

He hit the ball foul.

"Oh no." Hubert said, throwing the bat down, "strike three. It's your turn, Robert."

"What's that roaring I hear?" Robert said. "Does anybody hear that?"

Then the wind started blowing, just a soft breeze and you could hear a deep rumbling in the far distance.

"I believe it's coming up a storm." Hubert said.

About that time, we saw a flash of lightening and a crack of thunder all at the same time.

"Let's head for the barn and play." Hubert yelled.

We didn't waste any time getting through the bars of the fence, because it was already beginning to rain pretty hard. We barely made through the door into the barn when the rain really began to come down.

This was not the main barn; Dad just had one stall to the right of the entry where he stalled his horse in the winter months. After entering you had the option of climbing a ladder located on the left leading up into the hay loft or you could go through this little feed room where we kept cottonseed meal, dairy feed, crushed corn, and other feeds for the livestock. On the other end of this entry was the corn crib.

"What's this stuff?" Hubert asked, as he sifted his hands through the cottonseed meal.

"That's Dad's horse feed." Robert said.

"Let me see how it tastes to this ole horse." Hubert said as he dipped both hands full up and gobbled it down. "That's pretty good stuff."

I can't recall how much he consumed, but that ole horse liked that stuff pretty well.

After Hubert had his dinner of cottonseed meal we climbed up the ladder into the hay loft and began burrowing under the hay. It's a wonder we hadn't suffocated under all of that hay.

I don't know how long we played and cut up in the hayloft. After a pretty long time we noticed the rain had stopped. We climbed down from the hay loft and tried to get the hayseeds out of our hair before we went to the house for dinner. Mom had about the same things for dinner as usual, taters, beans, corn bread and milk and some kind of meat. This was the poor people's standard meal; but we never went hungry. The beans may be green beans, pickled beans, or pintos or the taters may be fried, mashed, stewed or baked. Today the beans were pintos and that was what Hubert liked best. We were all hungry and had our share. I think Hubert had second helpings of everything.

The next day was Sunday and we didn't get together to play that Sunday. Usually through school days we only saw Hubert on Saturdays. He went to Otter Creek School and we were going to Kyle at that time. When the weather was mild Hubert had the option of walking home from school or waiting until the last bus and ride the bus home.

If they walked they took the near cut across Otter Mountain.

On the following Monday evening, they were walking home.

Well Hubert started out to walking. He made it about a mile up on Otter Mountain when he took cramp colic and couldn't go any further. I think one of his sisters went on home to get help. Hubert was laid out on the road bank. Lloyd, Hubert's father, said, "I'll have to try and get him home somehow."

He picked up the little axe he used to split kindling as he passed the chopping block and some rope and a couple of burlap sacks from the barn and headed out to try and bring Hubert home. He found Hubert about a quarter mile down on the West side of the mountain. He was just folded up moaning and groaning.

"What happened, Son?" Lloyd asked Hubert. "What did you have to eat for dinner?"

"Just what they gave us at the lunchroom. I think it was mashed potatoes, coleslaw, a biscuit, and pinto beans."

I guess Hubert had forgotten about what he had eaten the past Saturday while playing ole horse. That cottonseed meal might have been hard to digest.

"I saw some birch bushes up the road. I'm going to cut a couple of them to make a liter and to try dragging you out of here." Lloyd said.

He was back in a few minutes with two poles about ten feet long. He laced the burlap sacks across the poles and made a litter.

"OK Son let's see how this is going to work out. Stretch yourself out on this." Lloyd said.

"I'm hurting so bad I can't move. Oh, Oh, I can't straighten out." Hubert began crying.

"Well you're going to have to help me." Lloyd said.

He finally rolled him on the litter and headed up the road with the two poles on his shoulders. He finally made it to the top of the mountain but he was so tired that he had to sit down to rest a few minutes. Hubert was no better; he just kept on groaning and moaning.

After resting a few minutes Lloyd picked up the poles to try and get Hubert home before dark. Going down hill was easier and with the gait picking up the poles began to sway and go up and down. Something happened to Hubert. He began to break wind. He was groaning and breaking wind with nearly every step Lloyd took.

"Oh, Ohhh, can't you slow down a little, Dad?" Hubert groaned.

"I can't slow down. I've got to get you home before it gets dark. Are you feeling any better?"

"A little bit, maybe if I could get all of this wind out I'd be alright" Hubert said as he fired off another round of thunder bolts.

Well, they made it home just as it was getting dark. Lloyd stopped with Hubert at the outhouse just before they got to the house.

"I've got to go." Hubert said as he made a dive for the outhouse door, just making it with no time to spare. It was good that the door was open. You could hear the blasts all the way to the road as the outhouse vibrated.

After about fifteen minutes Hubert came out.

"I'm going to tell Maw." Hubert snubbed as he walked on to the house, feeling much better

They never did figure out what caused this reaction. It must have been something Hubert ate! If Hubert hadn't been one tough little boy he might have not made it. Hubert was one of the toughest

I've ever known. By the next day he had rebounded and never knew anything had happened. He was always ready to play ole horse or anything rough and rowdy. Hubert liked playing games in the reality mode.

OUR SECOND SWIMMING HOLE

I think it was in 1945 or 1946 Robert, Hubert and I started our second swimming hole.

We had come up with a good place in our old pasture. It was ideal with grass on both sides and in the open sunshine. The location was just above where the lane runs from the present old chicken house barn to the branch and just above the clump of laurel that grows across the branch. The water was coming from a spring where Bateman branch started. The water just bubbled up from under a big rock about fifty feet above the place we decided to build the dam. My dad, Clayton, approved us building the dam. He said that he and some boys built one near the same spot when he was growing up.

He remembered a funny story about their pond. He said they had found an old door that they floated in the pond to play on. They would run and jump on the door and take a second jump to the other side. There was one catch to this you must hit in the center of the door on that first leap or you didn't get to make it to the other side.

One Sunday morning they were playing in the pond. Some swimming, some running and pouncing off the old door, and some just laying around watching; here comes one of the bigger boys from over on Long Branch dressed in his Sunday go to meeting suit. He just wanted to show them how the big cat did it. So he kicked it into overdrive from about fifty feet out and makes a flying leap for the old door. By this time the door had floated off center toward the far side and he hit the front edge of the door. The door flipped up and hydroplaned always up on the bank. What a splash! There wasn't a dry thread left on the big cat. All he could do was tuck his tail and return home to change clothes. These old hillbillies did have fun growing up in the roaring 20's too. Some times Dad would sit at the supper table and tell stories for hours at a time of the good times they had growing up. Mom would tell of the parties they had on Long Branch on Sunday evenings; playing blind fold, pin the tail on the donkey, holding debates and other games. Remember, we didn't have televisions to watch: but you don't have to have televisions and modern games to have fun. Poor mountain people didn't have much but life was good, very rich, we had one another. Live was more interactive with families and friends. As I look back to that time, I think life was more enjoyable than it is now.

Ok. Let's get back to building our swimming hole. We had built other ponds before this but they were just that, ponds. We decided this was going to be different. We all wanted to learn to swim. So we gathered up all the tools we had; shovels, hoes, mattocks, crowbars, axes and anything we could use.

We started off digging into the bank on each side to make sure we were starting off on solid ground. We found a white oak tree lap that Dad had left while getting firewood.

"Hey, look what I found." Hubert hollered from the edge of the woods. "Bring that axe over here and let me cut a few limbs off this thing. We'll drop it down in the slots we cut on each side. That'll hold it. That white oak will take the pressure."

That is the way our swimming hole got started. After we got started we had other helpers. I know that Jim Solesbee and it seems there were others that helped. I know for sure that Ole Crow was in on the whole thing. He was the chief inspector over the project. And after we completed the pond, Ole Crow, our pet crow, was the overseer of the dressing room "the laurel thicket" located about a hundred feet across from the pond where we changed clothes.

After getting the white oak lap in place, we cut stakes and sharpened and drove them in the ground against the log. Then some of the hard work began. There were a lot of big flint rocks that had to be moved. Some of which were probably two hundred pounds. It took all three of us to move some of them.

"Hubert, hand me that crowbar down here." Robert said. "We need to get these things out so we won't hit them trying to swim."

We dredged and moved three or four giants and a lot of smaller ones. We used these to reinforce the pond and also it helped make the pond deeper where we dredged these out of the bottom.

"I'm getting awful wet. My pants are soaked up to my knees." I s I noticed that Hubert and Robert were both wetter than I.

"I tell youns what I'm going to do. They ain't no body around here but us. I'm going to strip down to my drawers." Hubert said as he slid his pants off.

Robert and I did likewise.

We now were ready to start digging the turf from the sides and packing against the frame work. We tried to make it strong. At the base the dam was about six feet wide.

We packed it and laid on sticks and poles to hold it together. This project was going to take some time. At this time we only had about two feet of water but some of us were getting anxious.

"I know we have a lot more work to do and I am going to haft to be getting over the hill." Hubert said. "I think I'll hit it and wash off."

Splash! It sounded like hitting the water with a boat paddle as he fell off the bank doing a belly bust. It must not have hurt too much. After splashing around awhile he climbed out and his belly was as red as a beet. He put his pants on and started to put his shoes on.

"My socks are missing. Where's my socks? That mean Ole Crow has stole my socks."

Hubert said.

Upon checking all three of us had one or two socks missing. We finally found all of them. Some were hanging on the barb wire fence and some were hanging on nearby laurel bushes.

"I'll see youns in the morning. Maybe we can get some more help. I'll see if I can get Jim to come and help." Hubert hollered back as he headed over the hill.

The next morning about ten o'clock Hubert and Jim came to help finish up the dam. We all headed to the construction site. There were Hubert, Jim, Robert and I. Of course Ole Crow led the way. He was a little fuzzed up because Jim was not a regular member of the gang. They had just moved into Long Branch and Jim was not yet acquainted with Ole Crow.

We had all brought cut-off pants. So the first thing we did was to head for the dressing room that is the laurel thicket across from the pond. This was a perfect place for a bunch of redneck hill billy boys. There was a nice trail that the cattle had made as they went in and out seeking shade. And there were plenty of laurel branches for clothes hangers.

"Don't leave anything loose where Ole Crow can find it." Robert said. "Roll up your clothes tightly and stuff your socks into the toes of your shoes or they won't be here when you come back."

That was very thoughty of him to remember this. Even in doing all of this sometimes Ole Crow would run his head up into our shoes and pull out our socks. It wasn't any fun to see Ole Crow flying across the swimming pond with your socks or drawers swinging from his beak calking and squawking every flap of the wing. Most likely he would drop them off in the big apple tree down the branch about a hundred feet. This was the Granny Lizzie apple tree. Granny got nearly all her fruit drying apples from this tree.

Well, it's time to get back to the big construction job. After changing into our sawed off pants we began work. Jim and I cut turfs from the banks and passed them down to Robert and Hubert that were packing them into the dam.

"We've got a big rock on this side that is going have to come out." Jim said. "It will take the crow bar to move it."

He got out of the water and with several plunges with the bar got under the rock and swung down but it didn't move.

"I'm going to need some muscle power here, boys." Jim hollered.

"It's coming right up." Hubert said laughing as he jumped upon the bank and swung on to the crow bar with Jim.

The rock came rolling out of its socket. "See what team work can do." Jim said. "Now, don't let it roll into the water. We'll have to roll it around the bank to get it on the dam. If it ever gets into the water, we will never lift it to the top of the dam."

It took all men on deck to get that boulder rolled into place on the dam: but it was worth it because it really added a lot to the strength of our dam and also made our swimming area bigger.

"Look here." Robert said, after we had piled in more rocks, dirt, and turfs. "It's getting deeper. It's above my straddle down here at the deepest place."

At this point the pond was increasing in size taking more water to make it deeper but it was inching up more and more. We were piling on everything we could find to build the dam higher. We went to the lower side of the dam and gathered up all the rocks, moss and anything we could find to shore up against the dam. We wanted it to be strong enough to stand the pressure. There was a lot of water above that dam and the pressure was increasing all the time. We now had the top log covered over with dirt, rocks, and turf that we had dug from the sides of the banks.

"If this thing fills to the top, it'll be four feet deep." I said. "That's deep enough to swim in. Hey, we'll probably need an overflow pipe. We'll have to see what we can come up with."

At this time it was about three and one half feet deep. As I recall when it was full it was up under my arms. We more or less just watched it fill up the rest of the evening. We were too tired to try learning to swim very much after all the hard work. We were all rather proud of our accomplishment. We were going to have a lot of upkeep and maybe do a few more things but we had achieved basically what we had set out to do.

By the time we ran down all our shorts, socks and stuff and get changed into our regular clothes, would be time to do up the evening chores. We just left our cut-off pants hanging on laurel bushes. Ole crow was talking fiercely. Or should we say just trying to talk. As we came out of the laurel dressing room and started back across the pasture, Ole Crow came sailing by me and took Jim in the side of the head knocking his hair all to one side.

"What was that?" Jim said as he jerked around to see what happened.

Ole Crow lit on a fence post and began trying to tell us about it. But it was all crow language No one was able to interpret what he said.

Hubert and Jim went on over through Bateman Gap to their home on Long Branch. Robert and I had to do the chores such as feeding the cattle, milking, feeding the hogs and chickens and getting in cooking wood. Children growing up in the mountains of Western North Carolina were given chores and responsibilities. Our free time came after these chores were done. Allowances were when Dad was lenient when we forgot to follow orders, he would allow us to take the lantern and finish the chore. After we finished we were ready to drop.

If the old Philco battery radio had enough life left in it, we might get to listen to the Lone Ranger. That was the favorite of all the boys. What a thrill to hear, "From out of the pass came the thundering hoof beats of the great horse Silver. The Lone Ranger rides again." I can still hear it today. These are a few of the memories we still have of growing up in the mountains from the early forties through early fifties.

Well, we had planned to try out the new swimming hole the next day. As the morning warmed up about ten thirty Hubert and Jim showed up and also Jack, Jim's younger brother, came along with Jim.

"Hello Jack." I said. "Where'd you get that cap?"

Jack had a real nice white cap with a long green sun visor bill, really nice.

"Shirda got for me somewhere."

Now I think Ole Crow liked the looks of that cap too. I noticed that he really had his eye on it.

"I'm ready to take a look at that swimming hole." Hubert said with that little silly grin on. "It ought to be filled up by now."

So we all headed out in that direction to the swimming hole. Ole Crow followed along crowing all the way and talking crow language.

"Wow! Ain't that thing beautiful?" Someone hollered. It was that, very beautiful, completely full and so clear you could see all the way to the bottom. We didn't hesitate to head for the dressing room. Jack had brought himself a pair of green shorts. They matched his cap perfectly. He had them stuffed in his hip pocket. I think we were all so anxious to get in the water that we forgot about securing our socks and clothes the way we normally did. Ole Crow didn't mention it either. In fact he was real quiet. I don't remember even seeing him in the dressing room.

"Here comes the cannon ball express." Hubert yelled as he ran from the laurel out through the field. When he got to the edge of the swimming hole, he jumped as high as he could and folded up into a knot and then hit right in the center of the pond. I do believe he splashed half of the water out on the banks.

"Come on in the water is nice." He said with his chin quivering from the chills.

We all hit it kind of taking turns the water wasn't that cold after you had been in a little while. The water came up under my arm pits approximately four feet deep. This was plenty deep enough to learn to swim in. Jack even got his turn. As I recall none of us could swim at this point. Hubert maybe could hit a few licks. I think he had been going to the lake some when he stayed up at his Uncle Lee Duvall's. We all gave it a good splash that hot afternoon in late June. I was overcoming my fear of water, the first step in learning to swim. After splashing around in and out taking turns because there was only room in the pool for about two at a time, we got out and started drying off.

About that time we heard Ole Crow come out of the woods where the dressing room was. He was flying over the swimming hole carrying something green in his beak and calking and squawking every beat of the wing. Oh no, it was Jacks new cap that Ole Crow had found it and he was heading straight for the Granny Lizzie apple tree. We all got our clothes on as fast as we could; Jack was so bad tore up about his cap he could hardly contain himself. After we were dressed we set out to try to rescue Jack's cap. Ole Crow had left the cap hanging in the apple tree about twenty feet high and he was all fuzzed up and angry calking quarreling and trying to talk and maybe trying to mimic Jack.

"I'll kill that mean ole crow." Jack said picking up sticks rocks or anything he could find and throwing up in the tree at Ole Crow. This was exciting to Old Crow. He hadn't seen this much excitement before in his life. We threw sticks and everything we could come up with to try to dislodge Jacks cap. None of these seemed to work. It was in a place where you couldn't climb up and get to it. We finally found a long pole that we got up under the branch and kept shaking until finally it dislodged and fell out. Jack grabbed his cap and brushed it off without finding any damage. Ole crow finally settled down and flew off somewhere. Over all we had a very good time in the old swimming hole and many more as we used that place all summer. I learned to swim a little and I think some of the others did also.

We had a lot of good times just playing around the pool. One Sunday afternoon we were fooling around and found a piece of garden hose about four feet long. Hubert had a good idea.

"Bert, if you will hold up the end of this thing out of the water, I'll take the other end and see if I can take it to the bottom and breathe through it and see how long I can stay under." Hubert explained.

"That sounds like fun. I'll get out in the center of the dam and hold up the end of the hose." I told Hubert.

Hubert got ready and I took one of the hose and Hubert took a deep breath and stuck the other end in his mouth. The water was crystal clear and I could Hubert and he could see me also as I watched him sink all the way to the bottom. The hose was just long enough to reach the top. Only an inch or two was out of the water when he reached the bottom.

"Now I don't know how long he stayed down but it was a pretty long time. My legs began to cramp as I squatted on the edge of that dam; or were those little demons starting to talk to me. I slowly let that hose down into the water and I think Hubert knocked as much water out of that pond as he did when he done the cannon ball. It was like Old Faithful erupting,

"What happened?" I asked, without cracking a grin. "Did a crawfish bite you"?

Jim was sitting on the bank watching. He turned his head to keep Hubert from seeing him grinning like a possum.

Hubert coughed and spit and sputtered close to five minutes before he finally said, "I got water in there somehow. You didn't let that down in the water did you?"

"Now you were watching me. Did you see me dip the end into the water?" I replied.

"Boy, that's a lot of fun. We try it again as quick as I catch my breath." Hubert said as he blew the water out of his hose.

"OK. Let's try it again. Now I'm going to be watching you this time." He said.

"I'll hold it about two inches out of the water and you watch me." I told him.

Hubert stayed and he stayed down a lot longer than he did the first time. Was something wrong? I'd better check on him. I slowly let the hose down in the water. No, Hubert was still alive. He resurrected in the twinkling of the eye. He liked to have drowned me knocking water out of the pond.

"You let water in on me that time." Hubert coughed.

"I was getting worried about you since you had been down so long." I said trying to apologize. "I hope you didn't get strangled too badly."

Jim just lay on the bank and laughed.

Hubert sure was tough. Who else could have taken it like he did? And I don't ever remember him loosing control and getting angry. Now sometimes he might try to get you back, but would that not be expected after all the pranks that were pulled on him.

HUNTING BUMBLEBEE NESTS

Robert and I were coming back from Uncle Carl's and we stopped at Hubert's, just fooling around. Now I don't remember why we were over there, all of us boys were nearly as close as brothers. My brother Robert and I, Hubert, Eldridge, Kenneth, David and Bob Solesbee, which were Claude and Inez's two sons; Colen, Jim, and Jack which were Sheridan and Katherine Solesbee's three sons; Joann and Junior my Uncle Ralph and Ruth's two oldest; and Kenneth and Henry Uncle Dallas and Francis Solesbee's two.

This is about all the cousins on the Long Branch side of Bateman Gap that we played,

and run with. There were others but this is the ones that were close our age.

"Robert, I've got something I want to show you. Come up here to the cellar." Hubert said, with a little bit of excitement in his voice and eyes glaring. I knew right then something was up.

They had a root cellar on the North curve of the road and a few feet above the house. Lloyd, Hubert's Dad, had dug back in the road bank with pick and shovel approximately ten feet deep, six feet high and five feet wide. He had then shored it all up with split locust timbers and built shelves on each side for placing canned food, potatoes, apples and other items for winter storage. He finished it off with a heavy oak door that was recessed about a foot.

"Thay's a bumblebee's nest right in above that door." Hubert said. "And I've got me a good idea."

Hubert began to dig something out of his pocket. "Have I showed you my new knife Maw got me? I've been sharpening on it. I've got her sharp as a razor."

That thing was about four inches long, white handles, single blade. We called that a pig sticker back then. That's what the old farmers used to cut the pigs throat when they slaughtered hogs.

"I think if you will peck on that board I can hold my knife where them bumblebees come out of that crack and cut their heads off as they come out." Hubert said. All the while he was grinning and laughing.

Hubert didn't say but I wonder now if he didn't have in mind to kill all of those bees and get their honey. Hubert loved bumblebee honey.

"We'll try it and see what happens." Robert agreed but I noticed he had a little smirk of a grin. So I moved up the road about fifty feet to a safe viewing position. Hubert got in position with his knife blade beside the crack where the bees worked in and out.

"Alright here we go" Robert said as he pecked on the shoring timber. Nothing happened for awhile, and then out rolled a big yellow bumblebee. Hubert swiped with that pig sticker but he wasn't quick enough. That bee spied that white hair first thing and Hubert heard the buzz and didn't hesitate in moving. Like a deer he bolted out of that cellar and headed down the road. The bumblebee was in hot pursuit about two inches behind that cotton top that was flapping up and down in the wind.

"Heah, heah, heah Nance, heah Nance, whort, whort Nance," Hubert called and tried to whistle for Nancy his little white dog. He hadn't learned to whistle at this time but he was doing everything he could. He thought Nancy was wonder dog. I don't know if he thought his dog could run that bumblebee off or catch it. Hubert just wanted some relief but Nancy didn't come to his rescue and he went out of sight around the road and ran off in a weed patch, somehow escaping the bumblebee without getting stung. Now Hubert didn't get any bumblebee honey this time but he never gave up. He was determined to have himself some of this delicacy.

"Hey, where's my knife?" Hubert screamed. "I've lost my knife."

"Now, wait a minute." Robert said. " Maybe we can find it. Where did you leave it when that bumblebee bomber attacked you?"

"I don't know. I don't know." Hubert replied on the verge of crying.

Hubert wasn't in shape to think straight at this time.

"Let's go back up to the cellar and start looking there. That's all I know to do." Robert said.

When we got back up to the cellar, sure enough, there right in front of the door laid that bumblebee guillotine. It was right where the executioner had dropped it making a fast get away. Hubert was quite happy now as he put his happy face back on.

SUCCESSFUL BUMBLEBEE ROBBING

"Whooooooo, wheeeeeeee." It's Hubert coming through Bateman Gap blowing his train. In a little while he wound up down at the house.

"Robert, I seen some of them big yeller bumblebees watering up there in the ditch." Hubert said excitedly.

"Where at?" Robert said. Robert liked bumblebees as well as Hubert, but for a different reason. He liked to make little boxes and put the nests inside and watch them work, playing beekeeping. Hubert liked to eat their honey.

"Right across the road, in the ditch, where that little spring is, they are getting water and going right up the bank into the woods."

With that said we all headed up the short cut where we had been riding the wooden wagon to see if we could find a bumblebee line.

"Where are they at, Hubert?" Robert said.

"Over here in the ditch. See that one right in there. He's loading up."

We watched a few minutes and sure enough he made a couple

of circles. And up the road bank he flew and disappeared in the woods above the road.

"He's got a nest up there somewhere." Robert said. 'Tell you what we'll do, me and Hubert will go up there and maybe we can see where they are going. Bert, you stay down here and let us know when one takes off."

"Ok, there's a couple tanking up in there now." I said.

I think they left me to watch because they were bigger and could run faster to follow the bees. I didn't have to wait long before one started circling for takeoff. "Here she comes." I hollered.

Hubert was first in line, just a little bit back in the woods. "I see him. Here he comes, Robert." Hubert yelled. "He's headed up you way".

About that time Hubert hung his foot on a saw briar and fell down.

"I don't see him." Robert hollered back.

"Awe, I got tangled up with this old saw briar and fell. We lost that one, but we'll get the next one."

"I think one is taking off, now, Hubert." I said. "This is a big one. He should be easy to follow."

"Send him on up. Yep, here he comes. I've got my sights on him. Robert, he's headed your way."

"I see him. It looks like he's headed toward some brush over there. Right, He's landing." Robert said.

It seems something turned on in Hubert. He bolted up that hill, breaking limbs and bushes as he went. He didn't let anything slow him down.

"Where did he go? Where'd he go, Robert? Hubert said gasping for breath.

"You see that ole tree lap over there? He went into the leaves right by that log." Robert explained. "Keep your eye on that spot and we will see if another one comes in."

I had arrived by this time but I don't think anyone even noticed. All eyes were glued on that little spot by the log.

I think that tree lap was where Dad had cut down an oak tree the year before while getting the winter firewood. That little ridge seemed to grow those Spanish oaks real well. Dad liked to cut this species because it split real easy. I now wonder how he managed to keep wood. It took a lot of wood. And we had to cut wood for Granny Lizzie too most the time.

"Here comes another one. Now everybody watch and see where he goes." Robert said. Every eye turned to that spot beside the log as the big "yeller bumblebee" made his landing and crawled through a little hole down into the leaves.

"That's where his nest is." Hubert slurred. I believe he could already taste that bumbler honey. "How are we going to get him out of there?"

"If you had a pole long enough, you could hide behind that big tree over there and gouge the nest out." Robert said.

"Sounds like a plan to me." Hubert was already looking for a pole. It didn't take long for him to find one either. In less than five minutes he came around the hill pulling the branches off a pole that was about ten or twelve feet long.

"That'll do fine." Robert said.

In no time flat Hubert was behind that tree gouging and

flipping those leaves back. Robert didn't have to tell me to take cover I already knew that those bumblebees were mean especially when you were trying to get their honey. Robert and I took up a position to watch at a safe distance. I don't ever remember seeing a bumblebee nest that strong. There must have been ten or twelve bees in that nest. Hubert was lucky they never did spot him behind that tree. In a few minutes, he flipped something up out of those leaves.

"I think I got it." Hubert screamed. "I'm getting tired; this pole is getting awful heavy."

He laid the pole down for a minute to rest his arms. "If I can stick this pole in that rat nest, I believe I could run off with it before they knowed what had happened."

Bumblebees always build their nest in rat nests. I guess they drive the rat or mouse out and build their nest in their home.

"Well let me try it again." The excitement was building in Hubert's voice as he stuck that pole through the rat nest and flung it around and took off running. After running a safe distance, Hubert flung the pole down and ran a grabbed up the nest and began peeling the honey out of that rat's nest.

"Wow." Was all he could say as he held up a black ball of waxy stuff about two inches across.

He kept cleaning all the straw and debris from his treasure. I don't know what all was in that ball of wax; bumblebee bread, bumble larva, and a little honey? Hubert didn't care. He had been craving bumblebee honey long enough. So, he popped that whole ball of wax in his mouth at one big bite.

"Boy that's good stuff." He said between chomps and smacking his lips. He really liked it. I think Robert was a little bit let down. He didn't get any bees to put in a box because you must have the nest to get the bumblebees to settle in the box. He did get some bumblebees later on. That was another bumblebee hunt.

YELLOW JACKETS IN BEEGUMS

Hubert, Robert and I had all found some yellow jacket nests during the early spring and we hadn't bothered them. We were just watching them grow. As time went on Robert had the idea of gathering them all up and putting them into an old bee gum. So we went about collecting them all by burning all the flying jackets and then quickly putting their nests into the bee gum. We ended up with the bee gum about half full of yellow jacket nests.

Starting out you didn't see many yellow jackets working out of the hive; but in time as the jackets hatched out it became stronger and stronger. It wasn't long until they were like a hive of bees. I have always wondered how those jackets all got along in that one box just like one big family.

We had placed the yellow jacket hive right beside the road where we kept them aggravated by throwing and hitting the box with rocks. After awhile they were so agitated that you could just walk by and they would swarm out ready to make war with anything that moved. A chicken or dog or anything would get covered up by just walking by. We would shell corn and call up the chickens just to see them get stung by those yellow jackets. One of those little bees would light on that old hens comb and knot up. I don't believe that the chicken would give the jacket time to sting. It would twitch its head and sling it off before it had time to sting. We thought it was fun to watch them jerk and flop about trying to fight off those yellow jackets.

We were having such a time one morning about ten o'clock when we looked down the road and saw Miss Eller coming. Oh no, what are we going to do?

"Stop!" Robert said. "Don't throw another rock. Let them settle down."

We didn't throw another rock. We scampered behind the old wood house on the other side of the road and found us a peep hole to watch the action.

Miss Eller was moving pretty fast for an elderly lady. She was dressed in her usual dress, a long ground sweeper of a dress with long sleeves and wearing a sweater. She always carried a long stick to ward off dogs, I think. She was the kind that attracted the attention of dogs. Our dogs didn't even notice her this time. It may have been because they were asleep at this time of day. Well Miss Eller must have led a charmed life. Those jackets were really swarming and she went right through them, and if she got a sting, she didn't flinch. I could see them lighting all over that floppy dress but she didn't seem to even know there were any jackets there. She just walked clippedy-clopping right on through that swarm of jackets. She did turn her head a little when she heard three little rascals snickering somewhere around that old wood house. I think she mentioned to someone that those kids were laughing and making fun of her. That slowed down our devilment of that swarm of yellow jackets. I don't remember what we got into next but it wasn't anything good.

REVIVAL AT WHITEOAK

In the spring of 1947, after school was out our Pastor at White Oak Church Brother Carl Denny, said he wanted to begin a spring revival. He also said that he was led to have morning prayer and a short service for all that were able to attend. I certainly believe God was leading in his thoughts because there were a lot of youngsters about my age that were coming to the age of accountability. I was approaching ten years old at this time and there were several others between eight and sixteen. Some of which had already accepted Christ as their Savior.

I learned about this revival from my Granny Lizzie, Elizabeth Owenby Bateman, who made sure that I knew about this revival. Now Preacher Carl Denny was her Nephew who lived with his mother down in Briartown, about four miles from where we lived. I think this would have made Carl and me about second cousins. Carl never married but stayed home and cared for his Mother, Oma Denny. Carl had another Brother, Bun Denny, well known in all Western North Carolina, Pastoring in several Churches in the area. Both Carl and Bun Pastored our Church at White Oak Flats during their live time of service.

Granny Lizzie was, in my thoughts, a Saint if I ever knew one. I am speaking in Biblical terms. She loved the Lord. She loved the Church. She loved her family. She loved her children and grand children. Now I am sure she had her faults but not many in the eyes of a ten year old boy. I can't ever remember her ever scolding me, even if I did deserve to be and much more. I will not go into details on this subject now because I want to tell about this revival. I think you will understand what I am saying as this story progresses.

As I have already stated I was no angel before this revival or since either but this was the turning point of my life. I was lost but now I am found. That is the turning point that I want to stress. My upbringing by my family and things my parents taught me by example and the talks, and instruction, Bible reading, taking me to Church and so many others that I just can't remember, impacted me greatly. How would I have ever known I was lost if I hadn't heard it talked about around the supper table or at Church. Thank God I was brought up in this Christian environment.

My Granny Lizzie had a lot to do with this too. Now I was always prowling around late in the evenings or sometimes at night. Many times I would be at Granny Lizzie's and I would always pause and peep in at her window before going on in. I didn't want to interrupt her evening prayer. If she was down by her bedside with her Bible I would pause and wait until she arose. Then I would back down the trail and come running up and pounce upon the porch so she wouldn't know that I was watching. Now I know that this didn't just happen. No, there is nothing that just happens. I was being shown something but it took awhile for it to sink in. I realize now as I look back on these simple childhood experiences and realize how important it is for children to know that Granny and Paw do pray in privacy. To know Granny Lizzie was a praying Granny has always been a post I could lean on. And I can't help believing that she prayed for me.

It was after the revival started and I hadn't gone once to the morning or evening service. It was beginning to gnaw upon my conscience that I was lost. I was having a hard time getting to sleep at night and the same thing was bothering me when I awoke in the mornings. I needed to get saved or I would go to that bad place. I just couldn't get any ease on this and had been going on for some time.

Granny Lizzie would make sure to drop by after morning

service. "We had three more saved this morning. Carl preached a good message. Bert, I sure wish you would go."

I wanted to go but when two spirits are pulling in opposite directions, which one do you follow? The next day would be about the same. "James got saved this morning. Boy, we had a good service. Bert, are you going to go in the morning?" Not a lot of pressure but just a gentle persuasion. By the time I slept on it all night. No, there wasn't too much sleep. By the next morning I was ready to go.

"Mom I think I will go to the revival this morning." I told Mom.

"OK, I need you to pick up a few things at the store after Church." Mom said.

So, I walked with Granny Lizzie and some others. I can't remember who all but probably Patsy, Ted, and maybe Phyllis went that morning. I can't recall every detail but I recall where I sat in the old church house across the road. There was room for eight rows of pews on each side of the church but on the left side going in from the back there were three or four then a space of two were left out for the wood stove and then three more in the front. On each side of the pulpit were three shorter pews on each side. The left side was the adult men's class. The right side was the card class. The front seat on both sides was used for "mourners' benches" but more the one on the right side where the Sundays School card class was taught. That Wednesday morning, I think it was Wednesday; I sat on the left side on the third seat from the front, next to the Aisle. I don't remember Brother Carl Denny's sermon. He could have preached on anything or he could have not even preached. I remember after prayer I was on my way to the altar and I met a teary eyed Granny Lizzie coming to help and assist me on my way. I hit the mourners' bench on the right side, weeping and trying to pray and didn't know how to pray. I felt Granny Lizzie's arm around me praying her heart out. She had been praying for me and all of her grandchildren a long time. The Lord hears the heart more than words Anyway that was the way it was with me. I didn't know how to be saved. I only knew what I had heard around the supper table "Jesus saves and only He can save because He paid the debt of sin.

Now a lot of sins I had done in my past ran through my mind. I have thought a lot about that and I have never figured out how the Spirit can reveal so many things in such a short space of time. Can you forgive that, Lord? Forgiven, all is forgiven. I am forgiven. I am saved. I felt my burden lifted. I know He saved me and this is all that I could tell I really don't know much more except after this his sweet and glorious spirit moved in, something we will never be able to explain fully. I can remember the time. I can show you the place where the Lord saved me by his wonderful grace; but I know not the way nor do I know the how. But I'll tell you all about it in the bye and bye I know everyone experiences salvation in a personal way. Just as God made every soul a different person we all have a different experience of salvation. What I think is most important is to know that we are saved. When you lock in on to that in faith and you know when and where it happened and you will always have a landmark you can go back to when doubt and temptation comes knocking on your door. I have had to go back to that place many times and I am sure that everyone else also in a similar way has done the same. Now the old church house is gone and a much a better building has replaced it on the other side of the highway. I can never more return back to the little old church but I find myself wandering in the back door very often in memory. There are fewer of us all the time that can remember the old place and before long all memory will be erased but the real Church that was there will continue on forever because it wasn't the building but God's people that made the Church.

Many fond memories I recall were Church related. Revivals, prayer meetings and all the meetings and Church gatherings were about the only place we had to go in those days. I recall one incident when Uncle Harley first got a car and drove it to Church on Wednesday Prayer meeting and parked it on the side of the road across from the Church.

Uncle Harley was always a leader in Church as far back as I can remember. We all called him Uncle Harley. He was a wonderful teacher and leader of young people. He was always at Church. His job as a blacksmith allowed him to work at home a lot and if he could he was always there on Wednesday night to conduct prayer meeting. A lot of the Bible he didn't have to read he just quoted it from memory. He sung base in the choir. What a base voice he had. You didn't have to strain your ears to hear him. It seems I can hear him still. He announced his calling to preach in his middle age, although a lot of people called him preacher before he announced his calling. As I remember it was after one of those Wednesday night meetings that some of the teenage boys found some wood blocks and lifted the back of the his car and jacked it up until one wheel was just above the ground. When Harley cranked the car and gave it the gas, it just sat there spinning the wheel. He put the pedal to the floor and it still didn't move. He got out and looked but didn't see anything. He didn't go to the other side where the wheel was jacked up. He got back in and gassed it again. This time he had it wide open ninety miles an hour. The boys said we'll give you a push and when they pushed it slid off the blocks and hit the road running. That thing jumped about twenty feet with tires squalling and smoke boiling. I am glad there wasn't anybody in front of him because there was no way he could stop.

"Well sir I certainly don't know what had that thing stuck. Thank you, boys," Uncle Harley said as he drove off.

At a revival, I recall, several of the larger children were gather at The Dwight Water's store near the Church. We were standing on the porch just waiting for the church bell to ring. Some of the kids were having snacks. Hubert was having one of those "yeller dopes." Standing next to one of the girls, he cut his eyes over at her and said, "I'll buy you one of these yeller dopes if you will let me walk you home tonight. She never replied. I guess that meant no. Well you can't win them all but you can't blame Hubert for trying.

Now, more about my Granny Lizzie, I guess in my eye she was bigger than life. She didn't stay home all the time. She had sisters and kin down in Briartown that she went to visit frequently. Sometimes being gone a week at a time. I would miss her very much while she made these visits. She would catch a ride with the mail carrier, Olsen Grant.

Now Olsen was no ordinary mail carrier. The best words I can think of to describe him, he was a public servant and may I add one of the best. He would never say no to anything that he could do to help anyone. He ran a taxi service, pick-up and delivery service, pick-up and delivery of freight from the depot, and many other accommodating things that I can't remember all of them. Olsen carried about everything except gossip and that was one thing he didn't have anything to do with. He was just a wonderful person that everyone loved. Not saying we haven't had a lot of other good ones since Olsen retired but he is the one everyone remembers most. I guess it was that he served so long and faithful. On different occasions when I missed the school bus in the mornings, I would catch Olsen's taxi and go on to school at noon. I always enjoyed the ride on Olsen's mail route. He didn't whistle while I was riding with him. But in the summer months you could hear him whistling anywhere on his route because he used natures air conditioner by rolling down the windows of whatever he was driving.

Granny Lizzie was also a Blair product salesperson. She might have made a little monetary profit but, but I think that what she got out of it worth more than money to her was just getting to go around and talk to people. She always took next months orders as she made her deliveries. The product line she sold was household wares such as cleaners, different flavorings, spices, and etc. Sometimes she would get one of the bigger Nieces to go with her to help carry the goods.

Granny Lizzie was skilled at doing a lot of needle work. There were still old parts of spinning wheels around. She told me about things her family had to do growing up to be able to survive through the hard times following the civil war. They kept sheep for wool to make their clothes. After shearing the sheep, the wool had to be processed and spun into yarn. After this the yarn had to be knitted into clothes. She could knit a beautiful pair of sox, a sweater, toboggan, and other clothing articles. She never was able to teach me to knit; but I did pick up crocheting and a little bit of embroidery. She was a quilting fanatic. She kept huge bags of cloth scraps from which would evolve the most beautiful quilt tops eye has ever seen. I remember one cold winter she bought a small wood heater and set up a quilting room in the side room adjacent to the kitchen. We would get in there and quilt after supper. Phyllis, her granddaughter by her daughter that lived down Bateman road about a half mile, would spend the night and help quilt. I don't know how we could see by those old oil lamps. I don't think we got much accomplished. I believe Granny just liked to have those grand children around. She would always pop some popcorn and maybe have some other snacks. I think this was much better than watching TV.

Granny Lizzie always kept a few chickens; a few hens, a rooster, and sometimes some baby chicks. Back in the early years we had never put running water in the houses. Mom and Dad had to carry water from Granny Lizzie's spring which was about two hundred feet. We also had a spring box to keep the milk and butter. One evening Robert had went to get the milk and they heard him hollering and someone went to check on him and the old rooster had him treed on top of the spring box. Well the next time I went to Granny's I broke me a sprout about five feet long and when the old dommer-necker took a run at me, he was met with a surprise. I took a long swipe and caught him in the side of the head. That was all old rooster wanted. He ran off crowing and cackling, never to bother me again.

Years later Dad lost his hammer and sent me to borrow Granny Lizzie's. She gave me the hammer and I headed back down the trail. I heard something behind me and turned just in time to see the old red rooster in hot pursuit and closing fast. I already had the hammer in my right hand and I made a wild swing. I don't think it was luck but higher powers were watching over me. If I had been trying I could never have aimed that hammer so perfect. That hammer hooked perfectly around that old rooster's neck and he fell off in the weeds hopping and fluttering, finally coming to a rest just lying there.

"That's alright son, I have some boiling water in here on the stove. I will be right back. I will fix him for supper." Granny Said.

Before she had returned, the old rooster began make some squawking noises. Then he began to kick and suddenly he was on his feet, half dazed but able to run. By the time Granny arrived with the pot of water, the old rooster was about fifty feet upon the hill cackling and then he let out a big crow.

"Well it looks like we won't be having rooster for supper after all. If he had waited another minute I would have had him in the pot." Granny said laughing a bit. "It's alright son you had better get that hammer on down to you Dad. Come back later."

From that time on, every time that old rooster saw me he ran off and started cackling and crowing. I am telling these little short stories just to show the relationship I had with my Granny Lizzie. All I can remember of her just showed me her love and kindness she had for me and all of her grandchildren. She just didn't know how mean and naughty I really was.

One time her brother Buddy had come up from Briartown to see her and I decided I would slip up and listen in on their conversation. "I told you I was naughty." I moved up under the window and couldn't hear anything very interesting. So, I thought I would add a little action for conversation. I found an old wire lying under the floor close to where I was at. I straightened the wire out the best I could and slid it under the vertical batten board that had worked loose. I worked the wire through the crack and all the way in under the wall paper on the inside. Now it didn't take long for this to catch the eye of Uncle Buddy and Granny Lizzie.

"I believe you have a mouse trying to get in over thar." Uncle Buddy said in a course voice.

"Be quiet." Granny said, reaching for the stove shovel.

I shook the wire a little bit more and wham, bam. She hit that wall five or six times in a split second. No, I wasn't a very good little grandson. I just lay there giggling but very restrained for a few minutes.

"Well, I believe you got him." Uncle buddy said. "You will be smelling him in a day or two."

"I hope I do. Then I'll know I got him." Granny laughed.

I laid low awhile until things calmed down, and then I jiggled the wire a little more.

Buddy began to laugh a little and said. "I believe its mate has come looking for him. The shovel banged the wall again and again.

"Shorley that must have got him." Uncle Buddy said. "You are going to beat he wall down."

As I jerked the wire out, he said. "I believe I heard one run off. Maybe he won't be back. You must have got some of them." Uncle Buddy laughed.

"I sure hope I did." Granny Lizzie said. "Maybe we can get some peace now."

I decided to quit for now while I was ahead. This was enough for one day. I now wonder what it was that made me the way I was back in my early developing years of free ranging just seeing what I could get into. Was anyone else as naughty as I was? I seriously doubt if any ten year could have had such a devilish, naughty mind as I did.

Granny Lizzie thought I was little precious.

I helped her do a lot of things later on when I grew up. When I was about fifteen I helped put her water into the kitchen. I actually done most of the work, Dad did help some on digging the ditch.

She said. "I have this set of Funk & Wagner encyclopedias I will give you if you will put the water in for me,"

I said, "It's a deal." And I started working on digging the ditch every evening after school. It took a long time. I think it was about seven hundred feet of pipe that it took.

She bought ever thing I needed. I even built her a crude sink. It took me from late summer until late fall to complete the job.

Uncle Buddy was paying her another visit.

He said. "I am staying until this project is finished. I want to see this water run up hill."

Uncle Buddy couldn't understand that the water running off

the steep mountain would easily run back up hill until it reached the level of the head. I believe that Uncle Buddy had to go home before I completed the project but he came back later to see water run up hill.

I wonder if my grandchildren will look back on Paw Pa and see similar fond memories as I have of my elders. I sure hope they do.

END

CPSIA information can be obtained
at www.ICGtesting.com
Printed in the USA
LVHW100014141221
705936LV00020B/141